The Practical Busi

BUILD YOUR PROPERTY

BUSINESS

Improve your business planning; business systems;

outsourcing and management skills.

Just like having a business coach in your pocket!

David & Beverley Lockett

Orders: Please contact: support@business-academy.co.uk

Or

Go to the website www.business-academy.co.uk

You can also order via the email address support@business-academy.co.uk

ISBN: 978 1 83805890 6

First published 2020

Dedication

This book was started in 'normal' times and completed during the COVID crises lock down of 2020. This book is therefore dedicated to ourselves for supporting each other through thick and thin; through very good times and exceptionally hard bad times; through lots of laughter and tears, for 30 years together and still going strong.

Also to our children, Will and Freddie, for listening, caring and encouraging us.

Contents Page

Preface

Why have we written this book, where did our knowledge come from and what will you gain from reading it?

The Business Academy is the brainchild of David & Beverley Lockett.

David started life in the corporate world as a computer programmer, with a degree in Physics and maths what else would you do. He quickly realised that he would prefer the world of marketing so he moved into Product Management and Account Management. After a few years of chasing the corporate dream, he was offered redundancy from one of the major telecoms companies and ran for the door!!! Then started his long and ever-evolving life as an entrepreneur.

Starting in management consultancy he specialised in cost reduction and then together we bought a chain of dry cleaners (obviously why wouldn't you). Having taken a bookkeeping course, he realised that he liked the numbers side of the business so he re-qualified as an accountant. He worked in the industry for a few years and then set up on his own. The Finance Dept Ltd was David's practice which specialised in helping small businesses become more profitable. He had premises, staff, everything but it was not giving him the lifestyle that we wanted since it was largely based around his ability to do a lot of the work or to manage the staff doing the work. He then got into property (we had talked about it for years, but you know you need a push sometimes).

His property journey started with Serviced Accommodation whilst on Simon Zutchi's Mastermind course, David came top 5 for his cohort. He then sold the practice and concentrated on property full time since this gave the promise of great income and the free time that was lacking as the owner of a small accountancy practice.

Beverley, on the other hand, retrained to be a business lecturer whilst their children were very small, after many years working for medium and large businesses in a variety of roles.

After nearly 20 years of lecturing in business, she felt that she had a really good grasp of the subject. Beverley's specialisation when lecturing was change management and organisational behaviour, this means building organisations and teams to be as effective as possible, recognising the culture that exists in the business and when it needs to be changed. She has also had countless jobs both in corporate and public businesses in a range of positions up to and including senior management. Beverley is also an Assessment Expert – that's not just exams but how to improve teaching and learning through the use of assessment methods. You will see evidence of this as you progress through this book since there are loads of worked examples to help you learn about the subjects we are covering. She was always there helping and supporting David through his business ventures as well. so she has both a broad and in depth practical experience of how to build a successful business.

David & Beverley are both experienced business coaches and mentors, helping many property people improve their business so that they can scale them.

Why have we written this book?

Along with our son William Lockett, we have taken our property business, Red Door Homes, on quite a journey over the last few years. We have grown considerably using our combined business and coaching knowledge. We have developed a range of planning tools to help us and read extensively to support our growth in all areas of business. So whilst we have made mistakes (who hasn't) we have treated these as learning experiences and used them as motivation to push on to develop the business further. This book brings together all that experience, mistakes and all, so that you don't have to make them.

We recognised that many property people (in fact many entrepreneurs in general) were great at property strategies and being entrepreneurial but not always so great at the business aspect. That is where this book came from; our desire to help you improve your business practices, so that you could grow your property business, just like we have ours.

What will you get from reading this book? Well hopefully a clearer idea of:

- What the vision for your business is
- How to organise your thoughts and business to support scalability
- How to plan your business so that growth is scalable, sustainable and secure
- What areas you might need extra help or training in to ensure your business can grow

PART ONE

Chapter 1

What will this book show me?

Quotation

"The improvement of understanding is for two ends: first, our increase of knowledge; secondly, to enable us to deliver that knowledge to others"

John Locke, English Philosopher 1632-1704

Chapter 1 – What will this book show me?

This little book is designed to give you a quick overview of business fundamentals as they relate to property businesses. It will help you understand how some of the different elements work together so that you can improve your property business and management knowledge, as well as improve your business planning to make your property business easier to run and more profitable.

Beverley has lectured in business for nearly 20 years, specialising in change management and organisational behaviour. For those who don't know, that is how to get the best out of teams, how to get them to change and how to set up teams and businesses to make them as effective as possible. All vital information needed for growing an existing business. It's the sort of stuff that can make the difference between your business working well, and it closing down quite quickly!

David has had many careers, both in the corporate world and working for himself. After being made redundant from the telecoms industry where he was an account manager and product manager he initially became a business consultant. With this business, he looked at cost reduction methods for his clients. He then qualified as an accountant because he realised he liked numbers, so he then opened his accountancy practice.

Through his accountancy practice and networking with lots of property people, we both realised that, very few small business owners (and even some medium ones) had any idea (or very limited ideas) about the basics of business. Even if you have worked in a large corporate organisation, you will know about your section of it, but running and setting one up on your own requires a different set of knowledge and skills. This is because tasks are self-appointed when you work in your own business, and you might not be the best person to set priorities or organise systems to get those tasks done effectively.

We really should not have been so surprised. All you have to do is walk around your local town – how many cafes, shops, etc, have you seen open up and close within 6,12 or 18 months That is just the visible businesses with a presence on the high street. The figures nationally are a little more worrying in 2018 alone there were:

- 660,000 new companies started up and registered in the UK
- That is over 70 new businesses being formed every hour (we do like enterprise in the UK)

However on the downside:

- 60% of those go under within three years – that is 396,000 closing down
- 20% stop trading within just 12 months – that is 132,000 closing down

But why? How could you stop this happening to your business?

Is it that these business people are not passionate enough? Do they not work hard enough? Their products must be no good or else their ideas must be wrong, surely!!! The truth is even scarier than that.

Evidence suggests that the success of a business is largely predictable and is all down to good management practice. That's right, good management – it is not all to do with passion, hard work, luck or even skills in doing the job, rather, it is how good you are at managing a business?

That is a very different skill to managing yourself or even managing a team. When you are managing your own business you have to design and decide EVERYTHING – that is the problem, people are good at doing what they do best and not necessarily good at organising themselves, their business or their team.

Exercise 1

So, you now own some property and you are running it as a business. Let me ask you some telling questions:

Question	Scale
Vision, how well do you: • Know what you want your business to look like next year?	1 2 3 4 5
• Share this vision with others	1 2 3 4 5
• Talk about this vision	1 2 3 4 5
Communication, how well do you communicate:	1 2 3 4 5
• your vision to yourself	1 2 3 4 5
• your vision to stakeholders	1 2 3 4 5
• your requirements to your power team	1 2 3 4 5
	1 2 3 4 5
• your needs to your business partner	
• your needs to your life partner (if different)	

Time management, how well do you:	1 2 3 4 5
• manage your time	1 2 3 4 5
• become the most effective you that you can be	1 2 3 4 5
	1 2 3 4 5
• plan your time	1 2 3 4 5
• plan your business	
• plan your actions	
Business awareness, how well do you:	
• know what your business needs	1 2 3 4 5
• understand the needs of your business as it grows	1 2 3 4 5
• how to grow your business	1 2 3 4 5
• how to get to where you want to get to	1 2 3 4 5
	1 2 3 4 5
• work on and not in your business	
Problem-solving, how well do you:	
• solve problems effectively	1 2 3 4 5
• have the same or similar problems reoccurring	1 2 3 4 5

• learn from mistakes	1 2 3 4 5
• delegate	1 2 3 4 5
• outsource	1 2 3 4 5
• use your time	1 2 3 4 5
Total scored	

On a scale of 1-5 (1 being not good, 5 being brilliant) please rate yourself:

If you answered honestly and scored 115-125 – well done you don't need to read any further in this book, you know everything and already have the skills to build a big, successful business. If you scored between 80-110 then you could do with pointers to become more effective and grow your business. If you scored below 80 – you could do with a little help in understanding how to grow and manage your business so that it can be the success you want it to be. All of this is learnable, you just need to be ready to listen, understand and take action.

Gaining management skills about how business works and more importantly, how you can make your business work better for you, is vital to ensure that your property business is sustainable and, more importantly can grow in a secure and scalable way. You may want to do it for your pension or as a legacy for your family. So having your business still around in five years would be good – having your business grow and giving you the lifestyle that you want would be even better!

This little book can show you how to start on the process of becoming more professional and business-like in your business. That way you can scale and grow it far easier because you are working on efficiencies and not just putting in more properties and more time!

So this little book will show you how to:

- Understand your vision for your business and how this is key to driving the growth of your business to give you what you want
- Improve your general management skills
- Understand how to plan your property business through a structured planning process
- Improve your business systems
- How, what and when to outsource
- Understand business finances and what your accountant is saying to you
- Attract better tenants and investors

Working on and not in your business

So what do we mean by working on your business? Working on your business does not mean fire fighting all the problems that come along. It means you should be planning, considering, improving and generally working towards a scalable, sustainable and secure business so that the problems don't keep coming up and you end up with less fire fighting.

When you are working on your business you should be like a conductor, standing at the front of the orchestra ensuring that everything runs to the right rhythm. You should be allowing each aspect of your business (or the instrument sections of an orchestra) to come into play when they need to so that the whole piece comes together and makes sense for everybody.

So in business you should feel like you are the conductor of your orchestra - you should not be running around trying to play every instrument in the orchestra and failing! Could you imagine what live music would be like if you tried? So why do we do it in business? You must aim to be your own conductor and not the one-man band that you have become. This is what I mean by working ON your business – making it work for you and not just chasing the problems constantly.

A property business MUST have the 3Ss to be able to grow:

- Scalable

- Sustainable

- Secure

What do I mean by this?

Scalable – your business must have the ability to grow. This seems obvious; don't all businesses mean to grow? Well yes, but some business owners get in the way of their business's growth. Can you believe it? Especially in the property sector property entrepreneurs can attempt to do everything. If you do that then you are limited in the time you can devote to your business. we all have only 24 hours in a day and this is just one of the very limited resources we have. You can't get any bigger because you can't devote any more physical time and effort. Some property people need to get out of the way of their own businesses growth!

Now there is a technical difference between growth and scaling a business. Growth is when you are increasing the revenue (money in) equally as fast as you are adding the resources to enable that increase. You may have bought two or three properties already but don't seem to be making any more profit – that is because you have grown your business, but you are using up resources as fast as you are putting in revenue.

Scaling a business is therefore slightly different. This is when you are adding revenue (money in) at a faster rate than adding in new costs. This is normally down to automation or efficiency gains. So ask yourself, how can you automate or become more efficient to enable your business to scale – becoming more profitable – rather than just growing?

Of course, a lack of basic business knowledge can also prevent a business from being scalable. You may be a world-leading expert in your employed field, but that does not mean that you have all the skills and knowledge needed to run and grow a business. Very few people do, otherwise there would be lots of very successful billionaires!

<u>Sustainable</u> – this can mean many things, but I like the definition from <u>www.Investopedia.asp</u>. "Sustainability should focus on meeting the needs of the *present* without compromising the ability of *future generations to meet their needs.*" I like the use of future generations because most property people are in this sector for the long haul, they want to consider their children's' or even grandchildren's futures beyond just making a fast buck. So concentrating on sustainability means thinking long term, this, of course, means planning which we will get into in the next section.

The website goes on to explain "Sustainability encourages businesses to frame decisions in terms of years and decades rather than on the next quarter's earnings ... and to consider more factors than simply the profit or loss involved." This also brings in the long term aspect of properties. You are probably not in this property business just for the profit that it will make this month, but for what it will give you long term. You should be taking a much longer view of your portfolio than most businesses take over their assets. This also means being very careful in managing them and getting the most out of them both now and in the future – again, planning and management skills are essential.

Secure – to enable a business to be sustainable and grow it MUST be secure. To us, this means having enough cash flow for the day to day running of the business as well as having enough investor (either yours or somebody else's) money to bring in those new projects. Barclays Bank has identified seven reasons why cash flow is more important than profit in any business – and this goes for property businesses as well!

1. Cash flow can be bought but profit cannot – if cash flow is a problem then you can always secure a loan, overdraft or sell assets to get more. This can bridge the gap and allow for growth

2. Investors look at operating cash flow to see a business's potential – it is not just profit that an investors look at, but the whole picture, a business that has a good profit can still go under if the cash flow is poor!

3. Positive cash flow allows you to be proactive – this means you can train staff, recruit staff, pay to use

software that will help. It gives you more options to become the conductor and not the one-man-band. It allows you to get those efficiency gains mentioned earlier.

4. Cashflow is difficult to manipulate. Profit can be manipulated (think of some of the big corporate scandals of recent times to know this) but cashflow cannot easily be manipulated, so investors will look at this as a better indication of a business's health.

5. Good cash flow management is a good indicator of a business's health. For all the reasons stated above, this is a better indication than profit for health.

6. Bad cash flow could affect business credit ratings and reputation. In a business like property where you are buying assets on credit constantly, a good credit rating is essential, so protect it.

7. Despite number 1 on this list, if you have good cash flow you can avoid taking on extra debt, a business with fewer debts for working capital is good for the reasons stated above.

So for a business to be Scalable and Sustainable for the long term it has to be Secure!

Virtually all property people we talk to have a long term idea for their property business, they want to leave a legacy, to get out of the rat race or to build their pension. This means that the property business MUST be around and growing to give them these things. So it is important that as property business owners they learn how to identify when they are spending too much time working IN their business and not enough time working ON their business. All business and leadership gurus state that business owners need this very valuable skill to enable the growth (and therefore scale) of their business.

However when you move from employment into self-employment (as a property business owner) the good news is:

YOU ARE IN CHARGE OF WHAT YOU DO!

The bad news is:

YOU ARE IN CHARGE OF WHAT YOU DO!

This can mean that running the business can become overwhelming. All tasks are self-appointed because you are in charge of what you do. This is not easy to adjust to or to understand how to differentiate between what needs doing now and what can wait, what is helping your business to become more effective or is just a waste of time. You no longer have a boss to tell you what to do or what is important. You have to decide and we are generally not brilliant at it! This is because we are not experts in working this way – YET!!

Planning – why is it so important?

From our experience, too many business people just re-act instead of planning for the future they want and any success (if it comes) is piecemeal and may not be sustainable. This is strange because we all plan our holidays – even if you are a last-minute person you still plan where you want to go, how you are going to get there, what you need to do to get yourself there and what you will do when you get there. But it is a constant surprise that few people plan their next year in business.

Business books talk about planning five years ahead – I find this particularly difficult as my brain can't visualise that far ahead. We don't even know what government we will have then, so planning that far in advance is alien to us. We do however understand that we are in the property game for the long haul, it is a long term investment of our time and money, so yes, even we have an idea and vague plan for five years!

What we do find easy is planning for the next year – just like planning your holiday, you can plan where you want to be and what your business should look like in a year. It's a bit like making New Years' Resolutions – but reviewing them and sticking to them till the end of the year!!

Planning – how do you do that? Well, some people take what they want to achieve in 12 months, split it up into chunks and allocate each month a chunk. This is fine, it's basic, but at least there is some thought there. The trouble is that success does not happen linearly – and this is particularly the case in property. If you want six more properties by the end of the year and you plan to get one property every other month, by month four, if you haven't increased your portfolio at all, you are likely to get disheartened because you have not hit any goals. Don't worry, the work you have put in place will yield results in months 8-12 because property takes time. Sometimes more than 12 months! So, knowing this, should we not be more realistic and plan for that delayed and exponential growth?

I am not talking here about having realistic goals – do not ever limit yourself by setting 'realistic' goals. Just be realistic about the steps to achieving those goals, working out the plan and then working that plan, this stops you from getting discouraged.

<u>How planning works</u>

Start with your exit plan – Trust us, we will talk more about this later on.

Have a business strategy – that is not a property strategy but a business strategy – where you want your business to go this year, or the next three or five years. What do you want your business to look like? Having a strategy for where you want your business to be is so important. If you have a vague idea, it is better than nothing, but writing it down and sharing it is essential since it gets it stuck in your brain!

Break down the year into quarters – 90 days – this makes planning easy and gives you time to complete some bigger chunks of work like purchasing a property, or refurbishing to flip or building new homes before your next big planning day. On this plan you should also split up the actions so that you have some working ON actions and some working IN actions – both are equally important remember, but working ON can get forgotten all too easy when problems that need fire fighting occur.

Break down 90 days into 30 days – then you know what you need to achieve by the end of the month, anybody can work hard and focused for a month. Remember some working ON and some working IN actions here. ALWAYS have working ON actions!

Break 30 days down into weekly and daily actions – by breaking down where you want to go into 'action chunks' you can work your way through these realistic chunks and know that you are working towards your 30-day goals; 90-day goals; yearly plan and moving towards your ultimate 5 year goals. You just have to work the plan or realistic steps– it is that simple!

So why have we written this little book? To help you gain vital management skills and planning tools so that your business can give you what you want, in the time scales that you want it. So that you can learn a little bit more about how to make your business a success. Most importantly so that your property business does not end up as a statistic in the 'failed business' column of the National Statistic Office.

You might be asking, have you used these skills and tools yourself and what results have you got? Good question. We are not here merely as an academic, a theorist who doesn't understand what you are going through or how difficult it is to hold down a job you hate whilst trying to build a better future for yourself. We use all of the tools in this book regularly and we can truly say that without them we would not have had anywhere near the level of the success that we have had. Working hard is not enough, you need to work hard at the right things and if you want to build a great property business that is scalable, sustainable and secure you need to spend more time working on your business that you currently do. You cannot grow by working in your business all the time.

But Which Action Tasks are ON and which are IN?

It can be hard to decide which actions to take, which ones are working ON and therefore working towards your ultimate business strategy and which ones are working IN your business. Our time and effort is very limited and it is normally the most important, urgent tasks that grab our attention constantly..

You can tell this by your emails and texts – just scroll through them, either from your job or your business. Which are the ones that take your attention immediately on a Monday morning? Those that are most urgent on that day. Sometimes these communications can pull us in all sorts of directions and away from our main focus and tasks for the day.

So there has to be some flexibility – we are not advocating being so ridged with your tasks that urgent and important tasks get left, but you have to decide which needs your attention NOW and which can wait for an hour!! This is where the Eisenhower Matrix can help.

Ask yourself, how do you deliver the business your future deserves when there is too much to do in too little time? This can lead to anxiety and stress and that can then lead to lack of concentration and everything can distract you – all those notifications pinging at you on your computer and phone screen. How do you decide what to do in this situation? This also helps stop your brain from worrying in the night and causing even more stress for you!

Eisenhower (the American President) famously said that he had "two kinds of problems: The Urgent and The Important. The Urgent are not important and the Important are never urgent". This beautifully describes the dilemma most of us in business face. He recognised that to have good time management (and therefore have control over your To-Do-List) you need to be effective as well as efficient. We must spend time on tasks that are important and not just on those that are urgent! Here is the difference:

- Important – activities that have an outcome that leads to us achieving our goals – our business strategy if you will
- Urgent – activities demand immediate attention and are sometimes about achieving someone else's goal. This is tricky because there are consequences in not dealing with them, but you have to weigh their importance to your business strategy.

Now unfortunately for us, humans also tend to concentrate on what are unimportant urgent activities so that we can clear enough time in our diaries for our success – isn't this backwards? Shouldn't we be concentrating on our business strategy?

Here is the matrix:

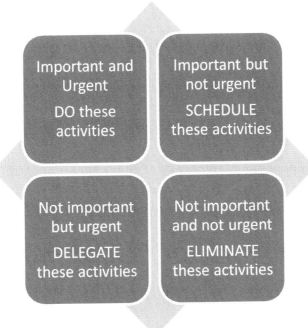

1. DO Important and Urgent – there are two types of tasks here, tasks that could not have been foreseen and others that you've left until the last minute. The last-minute activities can be reduced (almost eliminated) by planning. Leave some time in your schedule for the unforeseen activities – there will be

some each day, just don't allow them to take ALL your time!

2. Important but not Urgent – Schedule these tasks. These are the working ON your business activities that will work you towards your business strategy. Make sure you plan time for them and protect that time, they are important. Planning time for you to do these activities means you are working towards YOUR goals and will help reduce your stress levels.

3. Not Important but Urgent – these are the tasks that prevent you from achieving your business strategy, they are normally somebody else's timescales you are working towards. Encourage your team to solve the problem for themselves and delegate (outsource) as much as possible. If you enable your team to make decisions, then you're Not Important but Urgent tasks can be greatly reduced. This takes time and planning.

4. Not Important and Not Urgent – well then just eliminate these as they are a distraction. Don't just ignore them completely – can somebody else do them? Again consider your team and outsourcing.

This little matrix can help you focus on your priorities – the tasks which will move your business forward towards its desired outcome. It forces you to be more focused on your priorities – in working ON your business and not just IN your business.

Exercise 2

Consider your To-Do-List for the next week for either your job or your business.

Think REALLY carefully about what is on it.

Decide which items should go into each section:

1. Decide how long it should take you to do the Important and Urgent tasks

2. Decide how long it should take you to do the important and not urgent – schedule that into your week

3. Look hard at the not important but urgent – how can you delegate these tasks? Work on developing your team so that these don't come your way again

4. Be careful about the distractions and try to eliminate them from your schedule and To-Do-List!

Background to our business

Red Door Homes was built on the founding idea of our son, William Lockett. David had already sold his accountancy practice within six months of starting a Rent to Rent Served Accommodation business, then 18 months later Beverley wanted to give up work, but the business wasn't ready, so she went part-time in her job to three days a week. William was not enjoying work (his boss told him to give up on property saying he could never do it and he did not want him advertising it on his Linkedin profile! Employers do think they own your body and soul sometimes). He lived in an HMO in Chichester (300 miles from home). His HMO was illegal and he ended up living with two men in their forties who were drunk or high most nights. We did not want our 20-year-old son living in these conditions and neither did he. He came home, joined the property business and we started Red Door Homes with a combination of our values and ideas.

So in two years we replaced William's income, replaced Beverley's income and replaced the Serviced Accommodation income (although we still have this business). This is impressive, even in property but remember it has been done in a sustained, planned way to reduce the risk for us and our investors. And we are still growing!!

How to use this book

Although it is a book you can flick through to wherever you feel you need more help. It comes in three sections to help you:

1. Values and Vision – how to understand yours. This will give you a much clearer idea of why you are in business and what you want to get out of your business. This helps to define your vision so that you can then share it.

2. STOMP – how to organise your business for better planning (and success). This is a framework to help you understand the different aspects of your business that will need considering. This helps you not only to plan but also to allocate responsibilities out.

3. Planning – how to work ON and not IN your business to grow it. This gives you a clear idea of actually HOW to plan – everybody says you need to

plan but are you doing it effectively? This section will help to break down the process for you.

There are simple tools, exercises and questions to ask yourself all the way through. It is best if you do the exercises, they are time-consuming and difficult in places but the effort will be well rewarded. There is also a Next Steps chapter. If you need more support, training or guidance then The Business Academy can offer help. See our website www.business-academy.co.uk

Chapter 2

Purpose, Values & Vision

Quotation

"Directions are instructions given to explain how.

Direction is a vision offered to explain why"

Simon Sinek Author and Motivational Speaker, Start with the Why

Chapter 2 – Purpose, Values & Vision

Purpose

"So tell me what you want, what you really, really want"

A good line from the Spice Girls but why include it? You have to ask yourself what you want, what you really, really want so that you can go and get it.

Tell me when you bought your last holiday; did you know what sort of holiday you wanted? There are many different types and we like our camping holidays in the middle of a French forest which is not for everybody, but we would not necessarily want a 5-star hotel resort holiday – we all want something different. We planned our holiday so that it gave us the rest that we needed as you planned yours. So you knew what you wanted from the holiday and then planned a holiday accordingly. This is just like your business.

You need to know why you have decided to go into the property business and what you think you want from it. This will determine your vision, which will guide your planning, which will end up giving you want. They are all linked.

Everything comes with some sort of cost. Nothing is pleasurable all the time. So which struggles or sacrifices are you willing to tolerate to make your dreams happen? You must have your heart and soul committed to achieving your dreams because when the tough times come (and they will come) it is easy to give up if your dream is not strong enough to pull you through.

What gets you so wrapped up that you forget to eat or drink? This is probably your passion, you get into the zone and forget life's essentials because you are enjoying it so much. Remember when you were a child how playing outside would be so much fun that you forgot to go home at lunchtime? I know I did, but what gives you that sense of absorption now?

What are you so fascinated about that you think about doing it all the time? What is it that you want to do? It is OK if you feel a bit foolish with these questions – feeling embarrassed means you are going against the herd, getting away from herd thinking – that will help you grow your business.

Find a problem you want to solve – we all like to feel like we are making a difference by saving some small part of the world. Ask yourself what property problems have you seen and how do you want to solve them? Sometimes the problems are not obvious, but they are problems, so you can help solve them and this will give you some purpose.

Passion and purpose are a result of action – the sofa is just too comfortable and is herd thinking! It will not develop your passion or purpose. To find out what your purpose is, you must take action. Go out there and find out.

Finally and this is the one that gets me every time – how would you like to be remembered? In the book The Values Factor, Dr DiMartini gets you to write your own obituary. Yep, that is one hard exercise to do, just try it. How would you like to be remembered? If you are not acting accordingly then you will not be remembered as the sort of person you would like to be remembered as so you are wasting your life and you need to change!

Exercise 3

Find 30 minutes, when you can be quiet and not interrupted. Now write down a eulogy that you would like to be read out at your funeral. Don't worry, you are not going to show this to anyone else so you can truly write from the heart. What sort of person are you? How have you made others feel? What will you be remembered for? If that person is not the person that you are right now, then you have to change and find your purpose. Change to be the person you want to be.

Values for your Business

You may have felt that the questions we were asking in the previous section were more about your values rather than your business values and you would be right. The two are strongly linked. Purpose, Values, and Vision are all strongly linked. Your values will be the tiller that will guide you through the sea of confusion towards your vision of both yourself and your business. You need something to help guide your thoughts and that is your values. Once you have them you can use them to help make decisions daily as well as the big planning questions – they guide everything.

When you are working with (instead of against) your values you enter the 'zone' this means you have more energy available to work for yourself, and when you are working in a full-time job which you want to get out of, finding more energy is vital – believe us, we have been there!!

Here is a 'Passion Circle' there are several you can find on Google but we like this one because it is for business. In this Venn diagram, you can see you need passion (your values are your passion); skills (obviously we all have skills we can use) and a market place (we need to sell something even if it is rooms, or houses to rent, or units).

If you have passion and skills but no market place then you end up being the 'starving artist'. You have all the passion but nowhere to sell the fruits of your labour. If you have a market place and skills but no passion you end up in a passionless job - I know this one well and it can be soul-destroying trading your time for money with no obvious way out. You can have a passion and a market but if you lack skills then you cannot convert that passion into something saleable, without sales there is no business – this is the situation for most of the failed businesses.

Too many businesses fall into this category because they lack those basic management skills needed. You need to be located in the middle of the Venn diagram – have passion for what you are doing, this means aligning with your deep values; have a marketplace to sell the products that your passion is creating and have the skills (including management skills) to make the business a success.

But the interesting thing about this circle is the passion – it's the passion that is driven from who we are, what are our deep-rooted beliefs and values that creates the passion. That takes some soul searching to find out. So here is exercise 4 to help you

Exercise 4

1. Write a list of 50 things you love – this can be anything

2. Write a list of 50 things you hate – this can be anything again

3. Rank both lists – what are the top 10 things you love and hate.

Normally they are mirror images of each other.

This will give you a real insight into what you value, try to avoid platitudes like 'integrity' 'honesty' try putting into words you would use daily. E.g. Hate – People lying to me; Being late; Being told what to do by other people. Love – Music; Creating spreadsheets; Designing rooms

Exercise 5

Write a list of 30 things you are good at and share this list with somebody you trust – It is often easier for someone else to see us as we really are so can they add to the list or do they agree with your list?

This helps us realise what skills we have and also what skills other people think we have. Very often something we take for granted is a real skill since other people find it difficult.

It is a really good idea to share this list with somebody you trust and who uplifts you. That way they can spot things you think are obvious or you did not realise about yourself.

When we did this exercise, David agreed with everything but said "you have missed off something vital about yourself that is important to our business". I had no clue what he was talking about. He said, "you take action, you just get stuff done". I said, "I just do stuff that isn't a skill". He then argued back for a while and explained that an investor would like this skill, anybody would like this skill. I am not sure if it is a superpower – it certainly doesn't feel like it, but I do get through a lot of work in a small space of time! It is important to share and talk about these lists.

Red Door Homes Values- an example

When we did the values exercise we realised that all three of us valued the environment, wanted to help people and wanted to have fun and respect everybody. This has been written into our promises for our business:

- Socially sustainable – our properties create communities both in the houses and the wider community
- Environmentally sustainable – all our properties are refurbished and run with the environment in mind. We have been accredited with the Green Mark because of our actions!
- Beautiful design – our house designs give a sense of community and are designed around our target market so that it appeals to them.

Along the way, we have fun because business takes up too much of our lives to not be fun!

Vision for your Business

Well, you now have a name, have the business registered with Companies House and are now a shareholder and a director of your own business, EXCITING!!! But what do you want to do with it? This is where you need to decide what your vision is. Your purpose will help guide you to build the type of business that you want; your vision will help guide your thoughts in the planning process as well as being something to share with everybody.

A vision is important because it defines the map that will help you get where you want to go and should motivate you when times are tough (and believe me, they will be).

Exercise 6

To help 'see' your vision, ask yourselves these questions:

- What does your future business look like?
- How big is it?
- What will it give you?
- What can you see?
- Who is with you?
- Where are you?
- What will your life be like?

These are high-level questions to get you thinking, remember nothing specific at the moment – that comes later. This is just to start the process of finding out what you want the future of your business to be. Once you have an idea of where you want to be, all you have to do is reverse engineer it to where you are at the moment. Only you will know how long this will be, but a minimum of one year, a maximum of five years.

Exercise 7

Now imagine what you want your property business to be like in :

- Three years
- One year
- Six months
- Three months (the next 90 days)
- Next month (the next 30 days)
- Next week (the next 7 days)
- Today – what do I have to do today to make everything happen??

This is the value of planning every 90 days – it gives you smaller steps that you can do every day working towards your BIG vision!!

The 'Vision' is for the long term strategic direction of your business, the 90 – 30 – 7 plans are for how you will get there.

There are no right or wrong answers here since everyone is different, but the more often you carry out this planning the better you will get at it, the more vivid your vision will become and the more excited you will get about achieving your vision.

The planning process is just the reverse engineering of your vision:

A vision of what you want your business to look like in 3 or 5 years

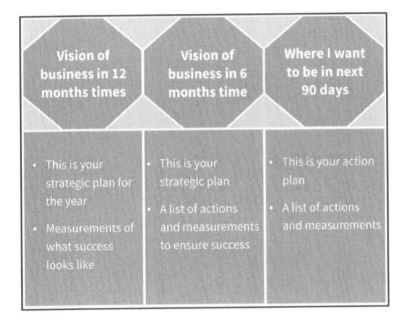

Vision of business in 12 months times	Vision of business in 6 months time	Where I want to be in next 90 days
• This is your strategic plan for the year • Measurements of what success looks like	• This is your strategic plan • A list of actions and measurements to ensure success	• This is your action plan • A list of actions and measurements

PART TWO

Chapter 3

Introducing STOMP

Sourcing

Team

Operations

Money

Promotion

Quotations

"Originality is nothing but judicious imitation. The most original writers borrowed from one another"

Voltaire, French Writer, 1694-1778

Chapter 3 – Introducing STOMP

What is STOMP?

Well, it is just a framework to help you think about your business. If you start your business off in the right way from the beginning it makes it easier to grow and scale. But don't worry if you have already started, STOMP will give you a framework that will help you understand your business better; give your brain a more structured way of thinking; and allows you to consider elements of the business that you might not be an expert in and therefore forget or worse, put off!

Big businesses organise themselves and spend time thinking about how the business should be organised and then developing and implementing the teams. So as a small or medium business, does it make sense for you to organise your business? If you spend time developing and organising it whilst it is starting out or while it is still small it becomes easier to grow and scale because the systems, processes and planning are already in place.

Using this framework will allow you to consider ALL aspects of your business – not just the bits that you are confident at. This allows you to either realise you need some more knowledge, or get expert help which in turn makes your business more efficient – using less money to make it run or run more effectively – using your time better.

So if you want to reduce your on-going costs AND be as effective as possible with your time then using this framework will help you and allow you to grow in a sustained, scalable way. We don't know anybody who is in the property industry for the short term, everybody we talk to wants to either leave a legacy for their family or pension or achieve a better on-going lifestyle. To get these things the business needs to grow and survive long term. This means that property business cannot be part of the 70% of failed businesses that are reported each year. Therefore property businesses need to survive to fulfill their purpose.

Creating a systemised business is also a more valuable asset than a non-systemised business, so you could create a business with a value beyond just the value of the properties that it holds, because a systemised business has an intrinsic value. This also has the added advantage of reducing your time input, and so creating a better more passive income for you.

Systemising your business means that you must look at all aspects of it. Michael Gerber the systems guru who wrote The E-Myth suggests having a systemised strategy for each aspect of your business and that is exactly what STOMP gives you, a framework to think of your business not as a whole, but as different departments working together. Once you realise that, then you can have a plan (a strategy) of how you will make each aspect more efficient with a system.

Now, Michael Gerber has enabled many very large world-class businesses to become more efficient, so why shouldn't you apply them to improve your business? That way you scale your business more easily because the work is not all down to you.

Robert Kiyosaki in Cash Flow Quadrant (the follow on book from Rich Dad Poor Dad) also talks about moving from being self-employed and effectively just owning your job, swapping time for money, through to being a business owner where systems are in place to enable you to grow. The next phase is then to be a completely passive investor where money works for you (and as property professionals, I am sure we all want to get here).

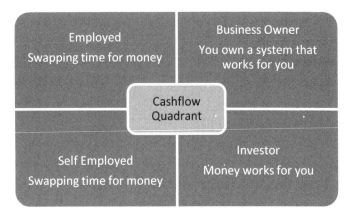

To make it easier to think and plan your property business the STOMP methodology breaks down your business into manageable units, just like a big business. All it does is logically organise the structure of your business, how every element affects all the others – they all interlock because they are all cogs in your business machine and they all need to work efficiently.

We will spend time going through each one of these separately. As you work through them you will see how they all interlink. There are cross-overs but breaking it down like this enables you to have a plan for each aspect, whether or not you are a specialist in it.

When reading the next few chapters consider how you organise and plan each element of your business and whether you need any help with the knowledge or skills. Remember that you are not on your own, help is here just go to Chapter 12 or visit our website www.business-academy.co.uk

Chapter 4

Sourcing

Quotation

"When you have to make a choice and don't make it, that is in itself a choice"

William James, American Philosopher, 1842-1910

Chapter 4 – Sourcing

This is all the lovely stuff that you learn on the property courses. What are you sourcing – what deals you want are affected by what you want to get out of your business. It comes from that purpose (which is why it is so important).

- If you want cashflow, then deals that produce cash flow from day 1 will be important to you
- If you want capital to grow, then deals where the value will increase will be important to you
- If you want cash flow and capital then, deals where you add value and then create higher returns will be important to you
- If you want a passive income stream, then deals where you don't have to do any work ongoing will be important to you.

Do you see? It all depends upon what you want from your business – what the purpose of your business is.

It also depends upon what your values are, there may be some deals that don't fit comfortably with who you are and dealing with people who do not fit comfortably with you. So, your values can affect the deals you go for as well.

You should have a vision and an idea of the Unique Selling Proposition of your business; these will also affect what deals you go for. What is it that makes your business different from everyone else's? Do the deals you are looking at fit with your USP, your vision and your values? If not why are you looking at it? Should you sell it on to someone else? See Chapter 9 for ways to discover your Unique Selling Proposition

All this is why the first few chapters of this book are so important, because what you value; what vision you hold and what you want will impact everything that comes afterwards.

Also, see Chapter 8 Promotion, because it talks about a sales funnel, and finding deals is just like a sales funnel. You need to have a funnel of opportunities coming your way. To grow big you do not want to finish one project and then start the process of looking for the next – as you all know it can take months to get deals over the line. Therefore, you should be working on your next deal constantly.

This book is not about property strategies, so please go to other publications and training courses for this – this is about what to do after you have all that knowledge.

Tools to help

Outsourcing can help to get direct to landlord or vendor letters printed and sent out. (see Chapter 5 for tips on outsourcing)

Sourcers can also be a good place to find properties because that is their area of specialism – ensure that you have a really clear idea of what your vision is to that they can find the most appropriate properties for you. Ensure that the sourcers are legitimate and have appropriate insurance. One with a good track record and reviews are best, ask them if you can chat with happy customers – if they don't want you to, then don't buy from them. Do some checking on the customers as well; remember you can search anybody on Google, Facebook and Linkedin and even check the contact details. Unscrupulous businesspeople could get you to talk to their 'mate down the pub'.

Exercise 8

How confident are you with your knowledge, and skills needed for SOURCING?

RED – not confident

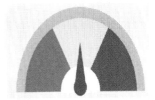

AMBER – a little bit confident

GREEN – confident

If you are RED or AMBER then you need to find some specialist help for this element of your business. This can be found in Chapter 12 or on our website www.business-academy.co.uk

Chapter 5

Team

Quotation

"A leader is one who knows the way, goes the way and shows the way"

John, C Maxwell, American Clergyman, 1947

No person will make a great leader who wants to do it all themselves or get all the credit for doing it.

Andrew Carnegie, Scottish businessman, 1835-1919

Chapter 5 – Team

Which sort of entrepreneur are you?

"I don't need to employ people I can do everything myself"

Or

"Help, how do I employ people"?

If you are the former you may be kidding yourself, because if you want to grow, you will have to employ somebody at some point in some form (might not be directly employed but we can come to that later). If you are the latter, well done, you have grown your business and you are ready for the next step, scale it?   But how do you take that step?

Ask yourself what does your organisational chart looks like? Now you will probably say "Don't be silly there are only X of us, we don't need a chart we all know what we are doing!" Well, I would disagree with you. Theodore Levitt at Management for Business Growth said:

> "All organisations are hierarchical. At each level, people serve under those above them. An

organisation is, therefore, a structured institution. If it is not structured, it is a mob. Mobs do not get things done, they destroy things"

Now, at Red Door Homes David had already been operating the serviced accommodation business for a few years when we started, he had recently sold his accountancy practice, he knew what he was doing. Our son William joined but didn't know what his role was, he floundered and flapped about without direction and we did not help him much (sorry Will). I was working part-time so was only working for two days a week in the business but was also struggling with my role and my place within the organisation.

David was used to being in charge; everything had to be checked by him. I did not have a voice and Will was flapping about with lots of energy and ideas but no outlet for them. Sounds terrible, doesn't it? Well it was and the thing that suffered most was the business – no growth, none at all. We could not go on like this, so we asked for help from a coach. They asked us to each take a personality test first. Then with some difficult conversations and LOTS of work on our values, we were able to decide something profound:

David should not be in charge!!!

This was shocking, surely David, who was the most experienced of us, should be in charge? Should be checking everything? Should decide on everything? Well, no, we decided to completely turn our business structure on its head. We put Will in charge! Yep, we put our 21-year-old son in charge of the vision for our business. This is our structure:

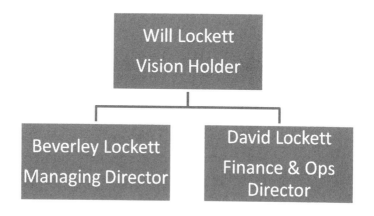

How did this make David feel? Well actually relieved, he was able to let go of the responsibilities that he did not like and were well outside his comfort zone and concentrate on what he did well. It was like he was a new person. It also gave Will a conduit for his energy and the opportunity to shine. It gave me the voice that I was missing and it added confidence and some direction for me personally.

We designed our business around our personalities, so that we each work to our strengths, meaning we all work within our natural flow and are far more productive! For those of you who know Wealth Dynamics, that was the test we did, there is a link on our website if you would like to talk to a Wealth Dynamics Coach and get yourself assessed, it is well worth it. Of all the things we have done to develop our business, this one has has the most profound effect and has been the single biggest factor in our success.

Name	Wealth Dynamics	Responsibilities
Will	Creator and Mechanic	Hold the vision; sources properties and investors; creates adverts Networks and is on the speaker circuit
Beverley	Star and Creator	Supports the team; on-boards tenants; project management; operates systems;

		designs living spaces. Networks and is on the speaker circuit
David	Lord and Accumulator	Runs the operation of the business; controls finance; runs accounts; produces and interprets business information project manages Designated driver for Beverley when she is speaking.!!!

David is much happier running the behind the scenes business. Will loves creating (finding properties), connecting with people and networking. He has helped to build the Red Door Homes brand! I prefer to be halfway between the two – using the systems, talking to tenants, communicating with teams and designing the living spaces.

Now, each of these roles is important – without Will finding the right deals for us we couldn't grow, without my designing eye we wouldn't get the rents we get, and without David controlling the systems and money we would not have the structure of the business. Each is important. We are very lucky that we have a mix of personality types in our business, but if you don't have a mix then acquire them through JVs, outsourcing or employing people.

It is just vital that you build your organisational structure around the personality characteristics available to you and allow people to thrive at what they do best. David loves talking to people, but it tires him out! When we were creating business cards we were asked how many we wanted – myself and Will said 500 each – David said: "I've never given out many cards can I have 100". This shows the difference in characters, Will and I will go and talk and swap cards and network, David will just talk and forget to get their details or hand out cards! Nothing wrong with either, but play to your strengths it makes life easier!

Outsource

Hiring staff is essential to business growth but should you outsource or employ? Outsourcing is defined as "obtaining goods or services from an outside supplier" this means that you could buy your administration from a supplier (a service) instead of employing somebody. Many property people have VAs which is a Virtual Assistant and this person may not even be operating from this country. A foreign VA is cheaper than a local VA, but it does have its downside.

However, some people may think that outsourcing will solve all their problems and be a lower cost to the business. This can be true, but you should also consider:

1. Control of your business

    Some business gurus say that "you shouldn't outsource anything that is core for your business" this is because if you outsource you have little influence over the outsourcer – they might not be operating to the same standards that you would do it to.

    So never outsource your competitive advantage!

2. Consider outsourcing activities where you lack expertise

If the activity isn't crucial and you don't have that expertise in your team then by all means outsource – you probably already do this. How many businesses have accountants or bookkeepers because they do not have the expertise to do their accounts (honestly you should anyway because there is no way you can keep up with all the latest legislation!). You would probably always consider hiring architects, builders, planning consultants – these all have specialist knowledge that you need on an *ad hoc* basis.

We also outsource jobs which we could do, but basically, it would be silly for us to do. For instance, we don't do the cleaning on our properties, we get professionals to do this; our time is far too valuable to be in rubber gloves half the time!

3. Decide what's best for your property business and consider the risks

Don't compare yourselves to others when deciding whether to hire or outsource – other property people may have specialist skills that you don't know about, for example, we didn't need a bookkeeper for ages because David used to be an accountant and did it as a way to relax. But, now we have grown, this can now be outsourced along with many other aspects of our business and David has found other, more fun ways to relax.

With employees you will probably have more control – this is because you will interact with them daily, you can check that their values align with yours at interview stage and you can set their priorities and goals to be in line with your business rather than their business. Remember a contractor is running their own business as well, so you may not be their top priority!!

Also, remember that an employee is a fixed cost and you have to have enough work for them to do otherwise that cost is not worth the money you are paying! If your business has a very large fluctuation in cashflow (like Service Accommodation) then you might end up with cash flow issues in the leaner months. But more on that in Chapter 7.

This section is linked to the Operations section very closely – if you have identified some processes that are not at your core and that you feel another person could do with little supervision then you should consider outsourcing them appropriately. If you have written out processes for them to follow this also becomes easier because they will know EXACTLY what you want them to do, when to do it and in what order. If you use some form of process here you should also be able to check that work has been done correctly and timely. This may be obvious if you have been running the process for a while, but it takes time and effort to pick that up without a written process, and we all know that time is money.

Many property people pass their social media postings onto others so that their profile can be raised and many people are specialising in this area.

Others find outsourcing the viewings of their properties to others makes sense because it will save them time. Of course, the full outsourcing service for landlords is an agent and a full management service – which for some landlords is great.

Others choose to use property sourcers to find their deals, this is a great way of leveraging other people's time, particularly if you don't have that time or expertise. However remember you have to ensure that the sourcers are finding the deals that you want, so they need to understand your values and your vision for your business as well. This is another good reason to go back over earlier chapters if you skipped the 'fluffy stuff'.

This chapter is also very closely related to Chapter 2. Here is a little story that perfectly illustrates, relayed to me as the COVID virus lockdown was first announced, of why you should share (with everybody but especially VAs) your vision:

"I always struggled to formulate my vision and frankly didn't see much of a point in doing that, considering I was operating on a small scale.

The past week made me realise many things about my business, including how much it means to me and what I want to achieve in the future.

Yesterday for the first time I shared those thoughts (so technically my vision) with my VA before she finished work. Today I woke up to an email from her with a detailed list of all the things she could think of to help us get through this tough period and grow the business. She clearly worked for a good few hours after her shift to create that. She started early today buzzing with ideas.

It's not like she wasn't working hard until then. But clearly, she needed something more than just a job description. The "why" was clearly missing for her.

I'm definitely going to put more focus on this from now on..!"

This shows the power of sharing your vision – you never know the extent of the true talent you have working for you unless you give people the opportunity to shine. Sharing your vision allows them to come with you on the journey. Sharing your vision is very powerful or as Master Yoda would say: "Very powerful stuff sharing your vision is."

As discussed earlier, there are some key roles within our business which we would not want to pass over. And these are mainly what gives us our Unique Selling Point – it is our competitive advantage. These are not only the core activities, but what makes our business unique. These key activities can be passed to someone else in later stages when your property business has grown considerably, so needs to be planned in. The planning required here is both for training in the way you like things done, your values and vision, but also when this should happen.

Employing

So when you are ready to employ somebody this is what you need to do:

1. Create a clear job description – this comes from the processes you have written earlier and should describe what you want your new employee to do. This will change over time but it gives them a clear

idea of what you want them to do and it enables you to think about whether you have enough work to employ somebody full, or part-time.

2. Create a person specification – this should highlight the sort of person you want. Be careful here, you can not specify what gender, age or any other protected characteristics! But, consider what qualifications or qualities you think your new employee should have. Again this helps to write any advertising material for the role.

3. Advertise the post – use a combination of the job description and the person specification to create your advert so that you are attracting the sort of people that you need as well as saying enough about the actual position. Remember to include something about where the business is going in the future (your vision) to give potential employees an idea of future opportunities for them.

4. Check that the new employee has a National Insurance Number and can work in the UK!

1. You are legally required to keep records for six years. So if you keep any potential employee's details – make sure they are safe and secure! These can be kept electronically, there is no need for paper here.

2. Agree on what sort of contract your employee will have – fixed term, full time, part-time. As well as pay levels and holidays etc.

3. Register with HMRC and note the key dates and tasks you need to complete. These will include sending payroll reports to HMRC; access tax codes and notices about your employees; appeal for a penalty and alert HMRC if anything is wrong. This can be outsourced to your accountant, bookkeeper or a specialist payroll company.

4. Understand your employees' rights, there are many statutory rights including terms of employment; pay; working hours; discrimination; workplace conditions (i.e. Health & Safety); pension contributions.

5. Get Employers Liability Insurance – it is a criminal offence to not have one in place on any day. It must also be displayed in your workplace!

6. Set up payroll system – your accountant or bookkeeper or a specialist payroll company could help with this and there are lots of software packages to make it as simple as possible such as the one built into Xero.

7. Keep a file – could be electronic – for each employee that should include: full name, address and contact details; emergency contact details; a signed copy of their contract; tax details; preferred method of payment; any other information that is important to them.

Although this all looks daunting your accountant and bookkeeper can help you. And remember employees or outsourcers are there to make your life easier but they can only do that if they know what you expect them to do and where the business is going so

share your vision for the business with them. More on how you measure success of employees in Chapter 10

To make your TEAM work you need to have people that have similar values or belief systems to you. This is not the same as characteristics or religious beliefs, but people that you will get along with and be able to work in the same direction as you. A poor choice here can mean you have an employee who may unintentionally damage in your business – you may even have been that person in your last job if you were unhappy. An unhappy employee can create havoc for you so be warned! Choose wisely and always try to understand what people's values are. There are resources on our website to help you here www.business-academy.co.uk

Communication

Getting communication right throughout an organisation is critical to its success. Far too many entrepreneurs grow without a thought of how teams will communicate, because you don't have to consider it when there is only you, or, you and a couple of others. However, the moment you start getting people working in your team, you need to design how you communicate with everyone.

This is of course not just about talking to each other – but how do you allocate work? How do team members know whose got responsibility for which part of the process? This is why having a written process is important. It allows team mates to know who is doing what, when they are doing it and when they will be finished. This makes life so much easier when managing a complex (or simple) project or multiple projects at the same time.

This is also about building the right type of culture in your business, remember you are probably building a property business to get away from a bad boss; don't let yourself turn into one! Bad bosses do not consider the culture of the organisation or the impact communication has on the team.

What do I mean by culture? Well an organisational culture is the "way things are done around here". You know from your job days, it is described as:

- The shared values of the business
- The norms and beliefs that affect the work
- The day-to-day behaviour (this can be positive or negative of course)

The culture of an organisation is reflected in the way new recruits are brought into the organisation; the way visitors are looked after; how the working space is organised (who gets the biggest space/office!); the degree of delegation and responsibility held throughout the organisation; how long employees stay; the methods and responsiveness of communication; how the team talk to each other and the style of the marketing material.

Have you ever worked in an organisation where the culture wasn't to your liking? I bet you didn't stay long, it is one of the biggest reasons people leave. Conversely if the culture fits with your values, you will stay longer because you enjoy it.

A friend of mine had the company taken over that she was working for, the new business owner's culture was really different and it was a shock for to witness the 'laddish' behaviour of senior members of the new business against the neutral cultural that had been in the original business. This made them stop and consider their future very seriously; could they continue working in this environment? I am sure you have been there as well.

If you run your own business then you 'set the temperature' of the business and therefore the culture as well. So be mindful and consider the culture you are developing – it is easier to build a good culture from the beginning than to alter a culture once it is entrenched.

Now you may be thinking there is only me at the moment and that is fine, but here I have been talking about your 'team' and team means more than just people you employ nowadays. Your team also means all the people that you work with to build and grow your business. This could be your VA, your builder, your accountant, solicitor, anybody who you work with or who works for you. So, when reading this section, think about EVERYBODY you interact with.

Getting the right culture in a business can mean:

- You release the potential for significant process improvement (if you have put the processes in place). Without the right culture, this potential will be lost.
- Attract the best talent – not only will you attract the best people to work with, but you will also keep them to work on the next projects. Remember finding good people to work with who understand your vision isn't that easy!

- You generate goodwill. What I mean by this is your team will be willing to 'go the extra mile' for you. You will be surprised at the level of goodwill good communication can give you, and that is unquantifiable in a business.

So how do you build good communication and therefore good culture in your business? It is a three-step approach:

1. Share your vision – this is one reason why vision is so important! If you have skipped over Chapter 2, go back. If you got stuck, then try Chapter 9.
2. Drive the right behaviours – this is all about what you measure to drive the behaviour you want. Chapter 10 will help here. In management, if you can measure it, you can manage it. But as Chapter 10 tells you, be careful with what you measure since this can also drive the behaviour of your brand.
3. Have good quality conversations – we will spend a little bit of time on this one now.

Remember; "It isn't what you said, it is what they think you said". Communications matter because they can be misinterpreted. When there is conflict, friction or frustration within the team then productivity will go down. Just think back to a time when this may have happened to you. I remember sitting in the Staff Room at College with everybody complaining, for what felt like hours, about the latest missive from management. How productive were we? Not at all. You know, you have been there as well.

So what conversations do you have with your team? Are they all related to performance; are they about meetings? Do you mainly use emails? WhatsApp etc? Do you give feedback or delegate tasks? It is important because they shouldn't all be about day to day stuff. You need to:

- Ensure that your team are motivated and understand your vision
- Ensure that your team are working to the best they can
- Ensure that your team have clear expectations about what you expect of them.

When communicating, it is useful to understand a little about the theory. The sender will code a message (write it) and then send it via a channel (email, WhatsApp whatever) this message will then be received by the receiver and be decoded (interpreted) – they will attempt to decode what you meant and understand it. It is only once feedback is given to the sender that the sender will know if the message has been:

1. Interpreted correctly
2. Understood and can be acted upon

Are your messages always decoded correctly? Have you ever had any misinterpretations?

Unfortunately for the sender of the message, there are things that can interfere with the message, mostly "Noise". This means what is going on around the sender and the receiver. You know the situation, you are getting annoyed because the dog has eaten your slippers, you send off a quick message to your builder. You builder is also having a bad day. The message wasn't sent with your usual tone of voice and the builder could take offence. As the builder isn't having a good day either, they are dealing with their own 'noise'. All this means the message doesn't get sent or understood in the way it was intended.

Be careful about this. Always think about how you are communicating with your team. Be aware of 'noise' around you (and possibly them if they are stressed on site etc).

Remember you cannot control every outcome, but you can control the way you react to them. This goes for the communication that you send out as well as the communications that you receive.

Data Flow

Just a quick comment about how data flows around your business. Every time data moves around so that somebody can use it, there could be an issue and it can get lost, distorted or changed. This could mean messages like the previous example or simply getting data to your accountant. Data moving around a system (your business) is always susceptible to errors.

Systems are the management of the flow of information. It normally fails when it is passed from one person (or computer) to another, or it is handled incorrectly or inconsistently. Having a process around the work to be done helps ensure that data is used consistently, correctly and the deliverables are maintained every time. This is why processes and system are so important.

For example:

Say you have asked your, maintenance person to go in and repair a broken toilet. They send in their invoice which says "Work Completed". This is not helpful because you don't know:

- Which property
- What work
- Whether the amount is correct

You can't, therefore, pass it to your bookkeeper because they will not know how to code it for your accounts. This is a failure of data flow across a process.

Think about how data is used and passed from one person to another in your organisation. Remember you can go paperless (we are) and scan everything. We even scan using our phones and WhatsApp is great to transfer material.

We also use Google Docs because it enables us to share folders so that true collaboration can happen. This is a fantastic tool.

Conclusion

Building you team means that you can grow quicker because they can do some of the work for you, however this does not mean employing expensive employees permanently. You can outsource and we are all used to outsourcing some specialist jobs (like planning consultants) but we need to get better as delegating smaller jobs as well.

Always share you vision with everybody in your team – this is important because how can they follow you if they don't know where you are going? They are effectively hitch-hiking in your business, they want to get somewhere as well but they are happy to use your business for part of the journey. Make sure you share the destination with them.

Be aware of the culture that you are creating for your team – it can be positive or negative depending on your point of view. You will attract people to you who share the same values and this comes out in the form of organisational culture.

Communicate clearly and concisely with your team – remember there is a lot of 'noise' out there that can interfere with messages. Always stop and re-read before pressing 'send'. Think "how will this be interpreted" only when you are happy should you press send.

Tools to Help:

For more help on Team go to www.business-academy.co.uk

- Using Google Docs
- Asana
- Evernote
- Dropbox
- TurboScan (on your phone)
- WhatsApp

Exercise 9

How confident are you in the knowledge and skills you need to develop your TEAM?

RED – not confident

GREEN – totally confident

AMBER – a little bit confident

If you are RED or AMBER then go to www.business-academy.co.uk to see how we can help

Chapter 6

Operations

Quotation

"Small business owners and entrepreneurs worthy of the title need to build systems that replace themselves"

Michael Gerber, American Writer 1936 -

Chapter 6 – Operations

Systemisation – why is it so important?

Thinking about Michael Gerber's quotation – can you replace yourself in your business? David once joked that he wanted to be the tea boy, just making tea and ensuring everybody was alright. This is close to the truth. You should be able to leave the 'day-2-day work' to people that want to do that, so you 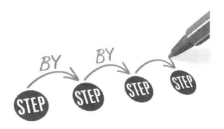 can just make sure they have what they want to do that work, the resources (in David's analogy tea!!).

We are always being asked why is it so important to systemise everything? Well, the short answer is because it can give you back time – and many property people got into property business so that they would have more time with family or friends, yet they forget to look at this area until the operation of their business is at breaking point.

Many business owners don't have a business model that works, but a model of the work itself. In

Michael Gerber's book, the E-Myth, this is described as the Technician's Perspective. The question they ask is, "What work has to be done?" This is concentrating on the day-2-day work and not the ultimate goal of growth or scaling the business. Michael goes on to explain how the Entrepreneurial Perspective is "How must the business work."

So do you ask yourself "How does my business work as a whole?" or do you ask "What work has to be done?" There is a difference, and it is a difference in how you think. If you are stuck in the Technician stage then you cannot grow or scale your business past your available time and this is a real stumbling block for lots of businesses, but particularly property businesses.

This is less to do with what's done in a business and more to do with how it's done. The true entrepreneur will attempt to get the how done correctly because that creates efficiency. That is where true scalability comes from.

Just imagine you have ordered something online from one of our big retailers – let's say Amazon. How quickly would you get confirmation of your order being placed, payment being taken or estimated delivery time if it relied on Jeff Bezos (The CEO) looking at all the orders and entering them manually? Of course, it is all done by systems and this reduces mistakes, makes it more efficient and reduces costs. The customer also gets a much better and consistent service.

What can Processes do for you?

- **Get back your time** – systems that are broken down into processes can handle much of the everyday mechanical stuff we do, which leaves time for us to concentrate on what generates revenue instead. Processes can also be handed over to others to complete, freeing your time.

- **Reduce mistakes** – having systems in place reduces the mistakes which humans, who are busy and have too much going on in their brain, can make (like you and me).

- **Maintain standards** – if everything is systemised, all your customers receive the same level of service whether you or an employee are operating the system.

- **Revenue generating** – because the 'mundane' tasks are done either automatically or done following a process, then your brain becomes free to be more creative and concentrate on working on your business and not in your business.

- **Business growth and scale** – systems allow your property business to grow because it is not determined by how much time you can spend working on it. They also allow you to employ people more easily because you already have systems for them to follow; they just have to learn them, or follow them from your descriptions.

All sounds good, doesn't it? You should be creating processes through your business to help realise your brain, so that you can work on your business instead of in your business.

To bring processes and systems into business there are a couple of rules you will want to follow:

a) Your processes will add value to your tenants, investors, suppliers, team, employees, JV – basically all stakeholders.

b) The process should be able to be operated by people with the lowest skill level (not because they are necessarily low skilled, they may be very skilled in their area of expertise but not in your process).

c) The process will bring order to chaos!

d) All the work will be documented – now this can be documented electronically and more on that in a minute.

e) The process will provide the same consistent level of service to all stakeholders.

f) The process will look the same from all angels!

Now you may have noticed that within the STOMP framework some things are interrelated, and processes and systems can relate to everything else. So, when looking at how to improve systems, look at the whole business and have a plan for improving ALL elements of it:

- Sourcing – this can be systemised
- Team – many aspects of this can be systemised
- Operations – virtually all can be systemised
- Money – lots of this can be systemised
- Promotion – lots of this can be systemised

Do you get the idea – you will need a bit of plan for how you systemise your business as a whole, but breaking it down into the different elements above can help it be less daunting for you.

So, what you are looking for here is a way of getting a repeatable process into your business so that it runs like clockwork – but importantly without you!

Documenting your processes

According to research, 63% of employees aren't clear about their business's processes. This is not good because these are the people that are supposed to be operating and running them like clockwork! Another problem in larger businesses is "who is responsible for them". This seems like an unlikely scenario, but if a business has grown considerably, the processes may have been there for a while and the original authors may not even be employed there anymore. This is also not good, but we can avoid these two problems by not only creating your processes documentation but also reviewing their effectiveness regularly.

If you can document your processes, not just document it but have the ability to check that the work has been carried out as well, then you are also protecting the intellectual property of your business. This could be part of your USP and you don't want to lose that competitive advantage if you have worked so hard to achieve it. Your team could decide to leave and set up themselves using all your systems. Having proof that they are your processes is very valuable.

The other part of actually documenting the way you want things done is to make it a lot easier for new team members to get up to speed, or if your team member is off sick, to still get the work done. How many businesses grind to a halt because somebody is off sick and their work cannot be covered? This problem is reduced if you have a documented process, since anybody can pick it up.

Being able to take a step back from the running of your precious business is very difficult for virtually all business owners. However, if you want to use the power of other people's time and effort you will have to, because you cannot do everything! This is about empowering your employees, or outsourcers, or team, it is not about control. Once your team are comfortable with the processes, then they can use them efficiently and possibly suggest improvements as well.

So here are the 5 IDEAL Steps to creating your systems

Step 1

Identify the thing you are going to systemise.

Pick something simple to begin with that you could systemise. It should be something that happens regularly, requires time and effort or frustrates you, that way you can see the benefits very quickly

Step 2

Design the process by writing down the sequence of things that need to happen in the correct order.

A well defined process will solve your issue in a defined sequential manner. I personally find post-it note and a large window is a great way of doing this.

Write each simple action on one post-it note and stick it to the window in the order they need to be done. You can then add things in when you forget them. Identify:

- The sequence of events
- Who is responsible for each step
- What information they need to complete the step
- What will happen once the step is completed e.g. who is the information passed to

- Does anybody need to check that the step has been completed?

Once you have a clearer understanding of the process 'flow' through your new system you can start to document it.

Step 3

Establish the documentation of your system.

If you have used our post-it note method you will need to write it down in a form that is usable by whoever is going to carry it out since a bunch of post it notes is not that usable! There are many ways of doing this.

At the simplest level a handwritten page may be suitable for your business but more likely you will want to use something like Word or Excel depending on what you feel comfortable with. You may want to create checklists to ensure that everything is covered; define forms that need filling in to capture information or even produce scripts for people to follow so that your business is always giving the same level of service.

There are some great websites specifically designed to help you document processes and some are free to use. One of the best is Process Bliss (https://processbliss.com), It is free to use for up to two users per business. We also have resources and modules on our website to help you at www.business-academy.co.uk

Completing Steps 2 and 3 for a simple process in your business will give you a really clear idea of what you need to do to systemise your whole business. It is just a case of starting and practicing - you will get better and quicker at it. The steps will also help you understand who is accountable for which bits and what information is needed at every step along the way. Once a system is documented it can be used by others. It is now repeatable so long as they follow the instructions that you have given them.

Step 4

Activate your System. You need to start using it. Don't be surprised if things take a little longer to start with. Whoever is using the system needs to get used to following a defined way of doing things (i.e. the way you want things to be done not the way they want to do things!). These will very quickly turnaround so that things happen more quickly and in a repeatable manner.

It is only once step 4 has been completed that you are working towards becoming a systemised business.

Step 5

Learn from your system. Once you have implemented a process it is important that you don't just forget it. Things change in a business and the people operating it may have ideas as to how to make it run better. You should therefore review each process every so often to ensure it is working well. If a process is not working well then it will get ignored and you are back to square one.

Of course all this takes time and effort, but just like putting on your email alerts whilst away from your office, it soon becomes second nature and over the coming years you will save yourself much more time than the time you invest to create your systems. How many emails are you saved from responding to by putting an alert that you are away for a few days? When added up that is a lot of time and effort saved for you. It is worth all the effort you have to put in to ensure that you can build a systemised business.

Remember you can systemise most things in your business. This will not only save time but also reduce your mental stress and stop problems occurring in the first place. Systems will also help to speed up your progress and most importantly enable your business to grow beyond the boundaries of you doing all the work!

There are lots of systems which can be automated with software packages, go to the Resources section of our website for our recommendations and modules to help, www.busness-academy.co.uk

There is almost no part of your business that could not be improved by putting some sort of process in place. There are many different ways to implement processes but another way of thinking about it is a simple three-step guide:

1. Capture the Process – consider the area of the process that you want to work on and what the process 'flow' should be.
2. Identify tasks – once the process flow is designed, then identify what task needs to be completed and design a checklist for those tasks.
3. Track progress – consider how you will track the progress of tasks, so that you can tell when they are outstanding or completed.

There are a variety of tools that can help you with each step. Exercise 10 will give you some step by step instructions to help you on your way as well.

Typical Processes

Here is a list of some typical processes that a property business may need. Read through them and decide which ones you already do, or which ones you should implement. When your thoughts are going in that direction you may find some other processes that you could automate.

Standard Processes	In Place	To Do

Sourcing
    Deal checking
    Landlord or D2V mailings
    Posting on Social Media		

Team
    Employee onboarding
    Employee offboarding
    Recruitment
    Team satisfaction survey		

Operations		

Tenant onboarding		
Tenant off-boarding		
Tenant satisfaction survey		
Policy review		
Maintenance visits		
Procurement		
Money		
Budgets		
Cash Flow		
VAT		
Payroll		
Promotion		
Publicity		
Investor Newsletter		
Promotional campaigns		
Advert maintenance, responses and analysis		
Strategic		
Strategy		
Competitor analysis		

Exercise 10

1. Identify activities that you do regularly – this could be to do with marketing, getting tenants, finding properties, social media, emailing, finance – paying bills, etc.

2. Break down each activity into:

    a. Processes – the actual step by step sequences of actions that happen

    b. Tools – any apps, websites or software that is needed to complete it

    c. People – who should be in charge of each step of the process

    d. Strategies – any techniques you can advise on how to complete the actions

3. Identify what you want your system to do for you? Do you want it to make things happen quicker? Do you want to eliminate mistakes? Do you want to make more money by reducing costs? Do you want to reduce workload and free up time?

Once you have decided what you want your systems and processes to do for you can then examine what you have identified in step 2.

4. So think about the activities and ask these questions:

    a. Processes – are all the steps necessary? Are they being completed in the right order? Are the steps in the process generating what you want?

    b. Tools – are you using the best tools and are they cost-effective? Is there another more sophisticated tool you could use instead? (This is especially important if it has been a while since you evaluated the tools you currently use, things move very quickly). Have the price of these tools now reduced – check your contracts and new suppliers because prices reduce all the time

    c. People – do you have the right people doing the right thing? Do you need to hire anybody else? Who could take on more responsibility? Could a VA help?

    d. Strategies – are there any strategies you could use to be more effective and efficient?

There is a lot here and systems are a big subject, but take the time to break things down. Do small processes first so that you get the hang of it.

I like to use post-its and a big window to work out how the processes should 'flow', like this:

1. Write down all the steps on separate post-its in the process

2. Put them in order onto the patio door

3. Add in who does what step

4. Add in what information is passed at each step

This gives you a simple process flow diagram that you can write up, and there it is! Your first process.

Tip: Start with something really simple!!

Always review your processes after you have put them in place. If you make changes always review the results. Has the change helped you become more efficient? Have you improved your profit margins? What has happened to your KGIs (Key Growth Indicates – more of these in Chapter 10)

Once you have reviewed your processes, look at ways in which you can improve them, always make improvements if your review flags up any issues. Processes and systems are on-going and are never set in stone, as businesses change constantly!

There are lots of process software tools to help you create the process documentation. As I mentioned earlier a good one we have used is called ProcessBliss - it is a free system for two users that just allows you to break jobs down into activities and it gets you thinking in the right way. This is not a natural way of thinking for some people, I have difficulty doing it, but once I have created one I can see its advantage and I have now created several new processes.

We have a brilliant person in our team, David, who creates most of our systems and has managed to make us very efficient and effective. We run not only HMOs but also serviced accommodation (SA) and The Business Academy like this because it is vital that we are as systemised as possible to be as efficient as possible. Operating SA is like running a hotel but on multiple sites, we have many guests checking in and checking out every day as well as having to delegate cleaning rotas amongst different cleaners in three different cities. This takes a lot of systems!

David has systemised this but still kept it so that guests feel they are being contacted by a real person, so we have not lost that personal touch. Here are just a few of the reviews we have:

"David thanks for the great communication and clear instruction before and during our stay. We had a great time and loved the apartment"

"David is an excellent host, he was quick to respond his description of the property was very accurate the check-in information made it very easy to get in."

All of this communication happens automatically without us doing anything!

If you are self-managing your tenants you should look at a system like GoTenant which systemises everything for you, from potential tenants booking viewings, through to tenants checking in and out. It is brilliant and has helped with the HMO side of our business. The tenants love it and it cuts down on a lot of paperwork, which is also great for the environment.

Conclusion

This chapter is only designed as an introduction to these topics, a way for you to think about your business in a different way so that you can improve it. If you don't know where to begin, just take a very simple task in your business and go through the 5 IDEAL steps to create a process. Just starting this will give you an idea of what is involved.

A really big tip is try to find short-cuts, apps, ad-ons anything which will make things easier and quicker for you or your employees. These can help to make you more efficient in the first place

We haven't even touched on the topic of Project Management which is vital for the operational effectiveness of a property business and many aspects of that can be systemised. It is a big topic, too big to be condensed into this book, but the same principles apply – just use the 5 IDEAL steps to start the process of systemising your project management as well. If you need help with Project Management there is a whole module on the website to help you as well as some resources for you to tap into.

Tools to help:

Process Bliss – this is easy to use web-based software that allows you to create processes and replicate and assign people to do them. You can then track if the tasks have been completed. It is a very powerful tool for outsourcing or home working team members.

Asana – Good for create 'to do list' but also projects plans and assigning work to other team members. Some features are only available on paid version.

Google Docs (for collaborative working)

The resources and modules on our website www.business-academy.co.uk

Exercise 10

How confident are you in your knowledge and skills to improve the OPERATIONS?

RED – not confident

AMBER – a little bit confident

GREEN – totally confident

If you are RED or AMBER then you need to find some specialist help for this element of your business.

Chapter 7

Money

Quotation

"A small business can survive for a while without making a profit, but if its cash flow dries up, the impact is fatal."

Theo Paphitis, British Entrepreneur and Dragon, 1959 -

"Beware of little expenses; a small leak will sink a great ship"

Benjamin Franklin

Chapter 7 – Money

How many times have you heard people say "I'm hopeless with numbers" or "I can't do maths". Well if you are in business for yourself, and you want to stay in business, you either need to get good at numbers or get someone in your business who is good at them. And let's face it, the sort of numbers you need to understand in business are pretty simple. The difficulty most people have with numbers, and therefore the numbers around money, is not the maths itself, it is what do the numbers mean and which ones should you be looking at.

The Money section of STOMP covers all areas of the monitary parts of your business. That means:

- Accounts
- Profit & Loss
- Balance Sheet
- Bookkeeping
- Cash Flow
- Income
- Direct Expenses
- Indirect Expenses

- Net profit
- Gross Profit
- Forecasting
- Deal Analysis
- Financing
- Interest rates
- Return on investment
- Cost of acquisition
- Asset financing
- Loans
- Etc, etc, etc

And the list goes on but a lot of this is very specialist knowledge but you need to understand the terminology and how some of these numbers work if you are not going to fall foul of excessive costs or lack of income. Obviously we cannot cover all of these sections in this book since this subject could fill many books by itself but we are going to give you a flavour of some of the key items that you need to understand when running a business so that you know what is going on.

Looking at the money side of your business can help you identify what your Key Growth Indicators should be. If you know your KGI's, you can then measure if you are hitting your goals for the next five years, year, 90 days or month. (more in Chapter 10 about this)

You can find a growing number of resources to help you in this section at our website www.business-academy.co.uk

What is Profit?

You should know what profit is – it is income minus all the expenses. Hopefully, the income is greater than the expenses which will leave you with money left over and therefore a profit.

But as a business person, you need to understand the implications of the equation.

Revenue	-	Expenses	=	Profit / Loss
(this can be called		(costs can be		Profit can be net
Income or turnover)		direct or indirect)		or gross or after-tax

How do you get more profit? Well, some would say sell more and you would be right (sort of) but what if your selling price was less than your costs for that unit. In general terms, the more you sell the more you lose. So not good. You could also reduce your costs but would that have an impact on the price that you could sell your product for if the costs are directly related to the product. If the costs you reduce are overheads like your mobile phone then that would be a more simple decision and definitely increases your profit. What if you sold fewer products but at a higher price? If your costs remain similar then you would receive more profit. But would raisng the price mean you sold less since fewer people could afford your product. Or would it just change the profile of the people who buy your product? This is called Price Elasticity of Demand and again is a subject in its own right but you can use your own judgement to come out with a good guess to see how it works. When we started our property business we decided we only wanted high end young professionals in our properties so we pitched the price at least 50% higher than average for the area. Local Letting Agents told us we were crazy, the market was saturated and we would not sell any rooms at that price. Well we had faith in our product design and we held our nerve. The first room we sold in our first HMO (Home of Multiple Occupation) was not an ensuite and it was the one by the front door. It did have a small additional room attached to it but we sold it for £700 per month when the local average for a double room was £425 per month. That is 65% higher than the average. [(£700-£425) = £275 higher £275/£425 = 65%]. So if you can sell your rooms for 50% higher per room do you need as many properties to make the same overall profit for your business.

There is more about this in the chapter on Promotion since it can have a major impact on your business and is another example of how all of STOMP is interconnected and is guided by your vision and values.

Do you know the turnover, costs, and profit for each property? What about each room? Each unit you create? If you know the room or property costs, then you can calculate what would happen if you increase your selling price. If you take on another few properties with similar costs what will happen to your overall costs? If it takes you to a larger scale business you may have to employ a property manager – and that would increase your overhead costs significantly. Is it worth it? Consider this question - When is enough, enough for your business?

If you have an empty room for two months, what will this do to your turnover and your profit? Should you offer discounted rent or a free rent period to fill the room for a guaranteed 6 month rent? What affect will this have and how much could you afford to offer? Voids are an interesting area to examine more closely since they allow you to look into the numbers behind your business, so do some comparisons over the seasons to see if there are seasonal patterns to your voids. Why offer discounts when the market usually picks up if you can wait for a couple of weeks.

Do you know which projects you have brought in on budget? Is your budget correct? Do you know if you are below or above budget? What does that mean for your business's cash flow or profit? Will you run out of money and if so when? So how much do you need to borrow from an investor and for how long and what rate can you afford?

All of these questions and more are important so that you can truly understand the key numbers for your business.

So, profit is the money that is left over after you have paid all your expenses – and that is *all* your expenses. Don't forget that individual units may be profitable, but what about the overheads of running your business, these are not allocated to individual units? This could include software costs, insurance, your salaries, offices, outsourcing costs. Lots of costs in a property business do not go against individual units.

You have to take these into consideration when thinking about your profit and what you can do to improve it. Remember, you can have cash in the bank but not be profitable and you can also be profitable but not have any cash in the bank! Profit is just an accounting concept, while cash is an asset that is in the bank! Let us explain;

What is cash?

If you are making a profit there will be money to spend, won't there? Well not necessarily, earning revenue does not always increase cash immediately and incurring expenses does not always decrease cash immediately.

How can that be? Well just because you have invoiced someone, they may not have paid you yet and just because someone has invoiced you for their work you may not have paid them yet. Both invoices will show on your accounts as a profit or expense at the date of the invoice but since no cash has moved it does not affect your cash flow.

Cash refers to money flowing in and out of your business. It is money that is available (or soon to be available) from either investment or direct business activity. It is there as a resource to be able to pay expenses. Profit is the amount that is left over after all the expenses have been paid.

Think of cash like water – you need it to survive daily or you will die. Profit, on the other hand, is like food – you can survive without it for a few days. Your business is the same, it can't survive without cash coming in but it can survive for quite a while not making a profit. Also, remember that you pay tax on your profit as well, so not making a profit may be beneficial for your business! However, to grow bigger and to have money to invest, you need profit (or your food) for long term survival.

We all know that you need money to buy and develop properties, and that requires cash. Most businesses fail when they are expanding because of a lack of cash – even if the expansion will create lots of profit in the future. It is vital that you have cash available to pay your expenses as they are incurred during your development otherwise it will grind to a halt.

But not all income and expenses show in your profit and loss which is another reason why you need a cash flow forecast.

When you borrow money from an investor the money goes into your bank account but it is not business revenue so it does not show in your profit and loss account, it shows on the Balance Sheet as a liability (since you have to pay it back at some stage). So it affects your cash flow but not your profit. Equally when you pay for a new property that you going to keep to rent out, the purchase of that property does not show on the profit and loss but shows on the balance sheet as an asset. Again, it affects your cash flow but not your profit and loss. The two other big ones are dividends paid to shareholders and taxes. Neither of these affects your profit and loss but can significantly affect your cash flow.

So as you can see, just using one of these tools: profit and loss; Cash in the bank or cash flow forecast does not give you a complete picture of the money in your business and is one of the main reasons why many growing and profitable businesses fail. They simply run out of cash without realising there was an impending, very predictable, problem.

So how do you ensure you have cash and not just profit?

You need to pay attention to both cash and profit for your property business to thrive and not just survive. So what do you need to do?

1. Have a plan of where you are going – this is your vision which was in Chapter 2. Know where you want to go so that you can get the finance in place before you need it. You need the cash (investment) to fuel your expansion.

2. You need a budget – know how much you want to spend on each room, and on each property and stick to it. This also gives you greater credibility.

3. Most important is, have a Cashflow Forecast – your accountant can help here, or there is a module on our website which can help at www.business-academy.co.uk. If you are showing a clear understanding of when you will need cash and how much you will need, it gives investors a more favourable view of you. You can also use the plan if

you have a lean period or organise more cash in the short term... Remember the lean periods happen when businesses are also expanding and cashflow will enable you to plan for this.

So cash in the bank is not profit and profit is not cash in the bank, you do however need both to have a sustainable, growing business. You do not, however, need them in equal measure.

Remember:

Vision starts a business (which is why it is Chapter 2)

Profitability helps a business to grow

Cash flow is the day-to-day life blood that keeps your business going

Setting Prices

Setting your prices is discussed in more detail in Chapter 9 but it is interesting to look at the prices that you are setting and consider what will happen to your cash flow and profit if you increase them.

What is a Cash Flow?

Money moves in and out of your business. In through investment, rents or the sale of units. If they don't pay on time then this can cause issues – anybody who has come through the COVID-19 lockdown period will know this can badly affect the cashflow of a business as tenants can leave or stop paying

Money also moves out of your business to pay expenses incurred.

Cash flow is the difference between the money flowing IN and flowing OUT of your business.

If your business is seasonal then cash flow can be really important – you have to learn to save during the good months so that you have the money available to pay expenses during the leaner months. This is one of the reasons why Woolworths failed – and other major retailers – they did not have enough money to pay their suppliers after a particularly lean period. Therefore they had no stock (and no way of getting stock) for the lucrative Christmas period. Result – no more Woolworths.

Here are some tips for improving your cash flow:

1. Control stock – especially if you are a developer or flip property business. Stock and the purchasing of stock is just money tied up in something you will not be able to sell easily. It is not an asset until you have completed the projects, added that value and are ready to make the sale. By stock I mean anything which ties your money up. It maybe properties if you flip properties or simply the materials you use to refurbish a single property.

2. Collect all your debts – always collect debts that you are owed. This goes for rent as well as any other services you offer. Money tied up in debts can very quickly add up and then you have no cash in the business despite showing a profit!

3. End unprofitable relationships – do not offer credit to somebody who consistently fails to pay!

Your accountant could help you build a cash flow forecast so that you can track your performance, and if this is not your area of expertise it will be worth the money! If you are happy with this area then there are loads of software tools that will link to your bookkeeping and your bank that will allow you to build a real time cashflow forecast. The forecast can show you what will happen to your cash if:

- Valuations do not go your way

- You increase your rent or prices

- You have to pay back investors

- You need more investment

- There are any seasonal effects on your business

- Or when you will run out of cash

You really should know what your cash flow is every month as a minimum, if you have a lot going on then you might want to increase this too weekly. It should be a working document or a real time tool that you use, not something that is static since cash is not static, it is always moving! If you only have time to concentrate on one aspect of the numbers in your business, let it be your cash flow, it is that important. It is the key indicator of the health of your business in the same way that blood pressure and blood flow is a key indicator of the health of your body.

There is a module on the website to help you create and use a cash flow statement. There are also pointers to various tools that are available for real time forecasting and further information on this vital aspect of your business. Please check www.business-academy.co.uk

What about your legal requirements around money for HMRC?

Do you know what information you, as a director of a limited company (making assumptions here, but you probably are), have a legal responsibility to report to HMRC?

Well, you should be keeping records about your company itself as well as keeping the correct financial and accounting records. The records of the company should include:

- Who are the directors, shareholders and company secretary (if you have one)

- The results of any shareholder votes and resolutions.

- The results of any Director decisions and resolutions

- Guarantees for the company to repay loans at a specific date in the future.

- Guarantees the company makes for payments if something goes wrong and it's the company's fault.

- Transactions when somebody buys shares in the company.

- Loans or mortgages secured against the company's assets.

You must share some of these with Companies House and store them at your registered address – if they are stored somewhere else then Companies House also needs to know.

Your accounting records should include:

- All money received and spent by the company (invoices and receipts etc)

- Details of assets owned by the company

- Debts the company owes or is owed

- Stock the company owns at the end of the financial year

- All goods bought and sold

- Who you bought and sold them to

- Bank statements and correspondence

Some of this information is contained with your accounting records and in your Statement of Income and Expenditure (or Profit and Loss as we used to call it.)

Annually you have to submit to Companies House a Confirmation Statement (previously called an Annual Return) confirming who owns the business. This just highlights any changes to your business, like the registered office or directors or shareholdings.

If you are a limited company you also need to file a Company Tax Return to HMRC and set of accounts to Companies House – even if you have made a loss and therefore owe no tax. This should include:

- Profit and Loss for Corporation Tax

- Corporation Tax Bill

Get professional help here since Corporation Tax is a complex area with many exemptions and allowances that require specialist knowledge. Without specialist knowledge you are likely to end up paying too much tax.

Tools to Help

Accounting software has improved dramatically over the last few years and many now exist which can integrate with other tools such as cashflow forecasts. These are invaluable to a growing business. We use the following because they are simple, easy to use and integrate with many packages and most good accountants understand them very well and can access them remotely to help you if needed:

Xero Accounting Package – Probably the best and certainly the most widely used accounting package on the market. It is superb.

Float – a web based cash flow program that links directly to Xero to help you create and manage your cash flow in real time

Banking App – use your own bank's app to keep on top of where the money is. If your bank's app is not good enough then swap banks! You should also link your bank to xero so your accounts are up to date in real time

HMRC website – This is stuffed full of really useful information

A good property accountant – Not all accountants are alike! You must find a specialist property accountant because they will understand the rules governing the industry in depth and be kept up to date with the latest information about property from HMRC. We use a property expert and it has saved us literally thousands of pounds over the last few years. Their contact details can be found on our website but whoever you choose, do your due diligence and make sure they really understand property.

Personal finance – There are a number of apps on the market to help you track your personal finance in real time with the minimum of effort. Keeping your own personal cash flow under control is as important as keeping your business cash flow under control.

Our website has a section of our recommended tools and contacts go to:

www.business-academy.co.uk/recommendations

Exercise 11

How confident are you in your, knowledge and skills of the MONEY section?

RED – not confident

AMBER – a little bit confident

GREEN – totally confident

If you are RED or AMBER then you need to find some specialist help for this element of your business. This may be as little as finding a bookkeeper to keep your numbers up to date or as extensive as completely building a new accounting system and finding a new accountant to get you on track.

Chapter 8

Promotion

Quotation

"The aim of marketing is to know and understand the customer so well the product or service fits them and sells itself."

Peter Drucker, American Management Guru, 1909-2005

Chapter 8 - Promotion

So you now have a business which may or may not be a limited company – depends what advice you got from your accountant. Please use a qualified accountant here and not 'the man down the pub' as the 'man down the pub' does not have insurance in case the advice they give you is wrong!! A professional will not only have the specialist knowledge to look at your situation and advise you the best way forward, knowing all the legislation that you have to abide by, BUT will also have insurance so if that advise is ultimately wrong and you lose money because of it, you can have some redress. This is called value and should not be seen as a cost!! Don't forget you are not paying an accountant for the three hours it takes them to produce your accounts. What you are paying them for is the twenty years that they have learned everything there is to know about your market so that they can advise you correctly.

Sorry about the rant, it is over, now but the value is a really important concept for marketing which is what this chapter is all about. There are two definitions of marketing:

1. The management process through which goods and services move from concept to the customer

    Or

2. Activities undertaken to promote buying or selling of products or services etc

3. Why two definitions? Well, I just like to get you to think – is marketing about having a concept and getting it to the customer (i.e. including all the R&D and designing the product) or is it just the buying or selling of products or services etc? You probably don't care, but it does depend upon what products or services you are providing.

Let me explain, as a landlord, are you just providing accommodation that can be a blank canvas for the tenants to do what they want with? Then the second definition is closer to what you want to achieve – just selling units. Or are you a landlord who looks at who you want to sell to; designs the units around what your customers will want and offers a service alongside. Then the first definition is closer to you.

Why does this matter? Well, it is all about Adding Value – the second definition doesn't add that much value to their products for their customers, they are probably renting them out at either below or market average to ensure that they have 100% occupancy at all times. This can be a race to the lowest price in looking for tenants. Not necessarily a bad thing, and probably a more traditional view of a landlord.

If you are designing your products –i.e. homes or rooms around the needs of your target customers then you are Adding Value to your product. That means that tenants will pay more for your product because it meets some need of theirs, i.e. nice designed rooms with splashes of colour, etc. If you then add in a bit of service alongside, then you are adding even more value.

Well, so what? Just as an example we add value to our shared houses through:

1. Designing the houses around our tenants – putting things in they want and making them a little bit nicer than the average.

2. Eco-Friendly – both refurbishing and running the properties in an eco-friendly way and getting Eco Accreditation from Green Mark along the way.
3. Socially Sustainable Houses – this is taking into consideration the social needs of our tenants as well as the wider community so that we do not sell 'little boxes' where tenants feel isolated, but that communities flourish within our houses because of the design, the tenants we attract and the way we run them.

So that sounds great but what does it mean? Well for probably about the same costs as refurbishing and running a bog-standard, magnolia shared house we can now sell our rooms for 50-60% higher than average. That is right! In one area the average rent for a double room is £425 and we get an average rent of £575 – that is a big difference and all because we look at how we can add value, this then comes across in our marketing.

Marketing Funnel

So who are you marketing to? Have you ever heard of a marketing funnel? Some of you will, but if you imagine a funnel with prospects going in the top and sold products coming out the bottom you will get the idea. You need a lot more prospects going into the top than fall out the bottom. Or, in property terms, you need a lot of people viewing your adverts to eventually have an applicant who will rent the room or house from you.

Of course, as a landlord, you probably have several 'funnels' that you need to consider. Let me explain, what does your business need?

- New Properties
- New Tenants
- Investors
- New Joint Venture partners
- New Contractors

Each of these should be thought about as a marketing funnel – how do you get people attracted to looking at you and how do you turn them into investors or tenants or properties.

Thinking about it this way you can identify how you can use different marketing techniques to attract different types of people. You should also be looking at how to add value to each type of person in each funnel.

For your funnel:

- Identify your customer (we will be looking at that in a bit more detail in a moment);
- Create a brand identity, do this not by expensive brand advertising but by aligning your values with your products (as discussed in Chapter 2)
- Develop your pricing strategy. This means not only considering all your costs BUT also the value that you are adding to your product. This is why the specific marketing definition you use is so important, more on price setting in a moment.
- Relate to your customers. This means really understanding the needs and wants of your customers so that you can align your product accordingly. This then should come out in your marketing material.

If you think of how you are identifying your 'customers' (or 'investors' remember these concepts are valid for whatever you want to attract); identify how you can add value for their needs, develop a pricing strategy that suits your 'customers' and then relate your marketing activity to them. This is how you get higher rents than average and more money in your pocket at the end of the day. It also makes your marketing far more efficient because you are only marketing to people who want your product.

Modern Tools

The marketing tools that you can use are now very varied and you should choose the right tool for your target customers (or investor). Consider where they will 'see' your advert and how you can tell them about your products. Modern methods, of course, include social media:

- Facebook
- Linkedin
- Instagram
- Snapchat
- Twitter
- Youtube

Don't forget these valuable marketing tools – especially as people use them all the time. Now with everything on our phones, you can contact people anywhere in the world at any time. The trick is to get them to come to you.

To get customers to engage with you, you must have a message which is:

- Consistent – you should be consistent in your messages. Don't confuse potential customers with different messages constantly
- Repeated – traditionally it was said that potential customers had to see a piece of marketing 7 times before they take action, this has increased to 11 times over the last few years – will your potential customers see 11 adverts (or touchpoints) from you?
- Have a call to action – don't forget this! Potential customers need to know how to contact you and what you want them to do next. This is really important!!! I have seen loads of adverts with no contact details or where a link is broken. What a waste of time, money and opportunity.

You may be asking, "when are the best times to post on the platforms?" So here is the latest research:

Linkedin:

11:00am – 2:00pm on Tuesday, Wednesday and Thursdays.

Wednesdays will give you the greatest exposure. Get together in a group to share each other's post and comment because the more you get, the more people will see it. We are in a WhatsApp group and we all share each other's posts to help each other. Monday and Friday have the poorest response, best to keep them for more 'trivial' questions which are also good for engaging an audience. But Sunday's is the worst day in the week for engagement. Not sure about Saturday's as it wasn't mentioned in the research, but that suggests it is not going to be good.!

Facebook:

11:00am – 1:00pm, Wednesday is the best, but you can get consistent engagement on weekdays from 9:00am – 3:00pm

Again Sunday's are the worst days for engagement and the lowest engagement is during early mornings before 7:00am and after 5:00pm each day.

Customer Avatars

A customer avatar is not a seven-foot tall blue creature from another planet or a persona in a video game. It is just a clear picture of what your 'ideal' customer would look like and helps you identify with your customer. A customer avatar is just as representation figure so that you can understand what drives your customers better. According to Forbes "you don't create your ideal customer, you discover it".

If you have been in business for a while, you may be very familiar with your customers already; however, if you are newer to property or this way of thinking, it might be new to you. A customer avatar, of course, does not have to just for customers (you might think you don't have customers, you have tenants so keep reading). Discovering the customer avatar for:

- Your ideal investor
- Your ideal tenant
- Your ideal purchaser

- Your ideal landlord (if doing R2R)
- Your ideal supplier

Wouldn't it be nice to have an idea of what your investor's wants and needs are so that you can market to them based on those wants and needs? Your investors are customers as well! So when discovering your customer avatars be very focused, the more focused you are the easier it will be. The more focused you are, the more likely you are to attract who you are focusing on.

If you are a developer, having a really clear idea of your customer avatar helps you to design your product around them. I have seen so many (new) kitchens and living spaces which have been very poorly designed, with little or no thought to how the products (units) will be used. Thinking about your customer avatar stops this, meaning that the units are of greater value to the customer. This means that they will pay more!

Examples of poor design are a kitchen in a one bed flat with space for a microwave (essential in all modern kitchens I am sure) but no electrical sockets anywhere near it. This, despite the fact that there was electrical supply in the cupboard underneath! It would have been so simple to add on an extra socket but very difficult to do retrospectively. Microwaves and spaces for them is my bug bear, I see so many newly refurbished studio or one bedroom flats designed for young professionals without the space for this basic requirement.

Here is a quick bullet list to help you identify your avatars (do this for each group you are doing!)

1. List what demographic they are in and any psychographic traits – write out as many as possible. Demographics mean explaining 'who' your buyer is – just the dry facts whereas psychographics explains 'why' they buy. Let's just look at some examples of the two:

Profile	Examples
Demographic "Who" your customer is	Female Aged 20-32 Single Working professional Income of £22+
Psychographic	

"Why" your customer buys	Finds fulfilment in career and friends Enjoys going to the gym Big fan of Pinterest Enjoys a healthy lifestyle Values time with friends Enjoys cooking

1. Just doing a very simple exercise like this can show you so much about your 'customer' and what they might find valuable and how you can talk to them in the marketing material. Using just demographics only gives you a fuzzy picture, using the psychographic element as well, gives you a much clearer picture.

2. Give the avatar a name (makes it easier to write) something like 'Ian the Investor' or 'Teresa the tenant'

3. Using the demographic and psychographic information, write a few paragraphs about your avatars and be as specific as you can; imagine them whilst you are writing. Who are they, what are they thinking when they interact with you? What do they do for a living? What are their challenges/problems?

What objections will they have to working with you? What are their values? What are their goals from the relationship?

The key is to be specific. There are some great templates out there if you wanted to go into this a little bit deeper. There is more information on this on our website www.business-academy.co.uk

Price Setting

One of the key parts of promotion is setting your prices right. How do you decide how much rent or selling price to charge? This can be hard; do you stick with market averages that are published in the magazines? Do you do some research and go a little bit above the average? Do you try and get quick tenants in and undercut everybody with low rents? Or do you go for high rents?

It depends upon who your customer is. That is why this bit comes after the avatar section. What will your customer (or tenant) pay for their unit? You must have a clear idea of what they do for a living and earn, so, what do you think they can afford? If you are aiming at blue-collar workers, there is no point offering a high-end product that they probably could not afford.

However, let's also consider Price Elasticity of Demand or PED. It is a simple little calculation that is taught in A Level Business, but is a very powerful tool that smaller business owners do not consider, let alone use.

Some prices are elastic – that means that if the price changes then demand will change by more. Consider a tin of beans, if it doubles in price, sales will probably drop by more than 50% - in other words, the price affects demand a lot.

Now consider petrol, this is more of a 'necessary' expense and therefore if the price goes up, demand remains high. Fewer journeys may be made, but everybody will still have to go to the shops or work, so it will still be bought. The price of petrol is 'inelastic'; the demand is not affected as much by a rise in the prices.

Now there is a lovely little calculation to go along with this, but don't worry I will not be showing you how to do it if you want to know, just google it.

Why am I explaining this to you? Well, this can be useful when considering what price to set your rents or prices at. How elastic do you think rent or house prices are? If you designed a nice product and set the rents high, would applicants apply and want to take a tenancy? This is some research that you will have to do.

But if you have designed your product around the customer avatar, you can attract customers who share your values (from Chapter 2) and you can offer them something that they need AND want (rather than just want), then you can charge an appropriate price. This is how we get higher rents than the average landlords.

This is a little bit more complicated if you are a property developer and building units, but the same principles apply. It is just that market trends will have a little more influence on the buying decision than for rented properties.

We are constantly being told by specialist letting agents:

- "You will never achieve those rents in this area" – yet we did

- "You will never fill an eight-bed shared house around here" – yet we have waiting lists
- "You will never get good tenants coming into this area" – yet we get great tenants

This is what Apple does so well, they have customers who are prepared to pay more for their products who are very loyal, just tell an Apple phone person that Apple are overpriced and Samsung give you more features for a lower price and see the reaction you get!!. Apple may not be the best, but they are the best at developing loyalty and *perceived* value for their customers.

Remember value or quality for customers does not have to be actual value or quality, just perceived. A test of perceived value or quality is to ask a group of people who has paid the most for a pair of jeans – they always rank between £15 - £150+ (the most expensive I have been told was £800 – for a pair of jeans, I fell off my seat at this point!!).

Well ask yourself, what makes people spend over £100 on a pair of jeans that are probably made in the same factory as the £15 pair and even made out the same material? It is a perception that they are buying quality. Normally this takes the form of a very small label with a certain name on it or a few bits of 'design' that actual cost very little extra in the manufacturing but add enormous perceived value so companies can charge far more. You know what I am talking about here.

Conclusion

Spending time and consideration on your avatars can reap big advantages for you, not only does it mean that you design a better product for them, but you can also save money and effort on marketing to the right people, in the right place and with the right message. That way you resonate with your customers and are able be much more efficient in your marketing.

Remember that the same rules apply whether you are marketing for landlords to buy their properties; to tenants to rent somewhere to live or to investors to invest in you and your business.

Tools to help

There are marketing, social media and customer avatar modules from www.business-academy.co.uk

Hoote Suite – for schedule posts on Instagram, Facebook and Linkedin.

Exercise 12

Step ONE

Identify your 'customers'. Write down who you are marketing to at the moment (here are examples):

- New Property deals
- New Tenants
- New Investors
- New Joint Venture partners
- New Contractors

Step TWO

For each of the above, write down what each of your ideal 'customers' looks like:

- What would they do?
- How old would they be?
- What would be their hobbies?
- What challenges do they face?
- What is important to them?
- Who makes the purchasing decision?
- (or any of the questions posed above)

This then helps you to tailor your product and therefore your message to their needs.

Step THREE

For each 'customer' identify at least ten places you could advertise to them. Why so many? You will have to get creative after thinking of five!!!

Step FOUR

Pull together some marketing material you could use and decide when you will use it. Having a timeline is important as you can repeat messages on social media several times to hit the person you want to.

Repeat Step FOUR!!!

Exercise 13

How confident are your knowledge and skills you need for PROMOTION?

RED – not confident

AMBER – a little bit confident

GREEN – totally confident

If you are RED or AMBER then you need to find some specialist help for this element of your business so check out www.business-academy.co.uk

PART THREE

Chapter 9

Planning

.

Quotation

"The most incredible businesses are started by entrepreneurs who relentlessly pursue their passion, but passion works best with a thoughtful, ambitious-yet-grounded business plan"

Charles Best, American Businessman

Chapter 9 – Planning

What is the point of telling you all about the STOMP methodology? Well, it is to help you plan the future of your business of course. Planning enables you to grow in a sustained way, as we discussed in Chapter 1, you have to be aware of and plan for ALL aspects of your business.

Now even if you are an experienced property business owner you can still feel overwhelmed by the number of things you have to keep on top of. Here is a little snippet from a very experienced (10 years +) property business owner about how they were feeling:

"The planning process overwhelms me, I have such a busy calendar and life, to put something in place seems too much. Planning is new to me and I can see the value, I want to make it part of my routine, but I am struggling. There is just one big empty page at the moment, feels like I'm starting at a cliff face".

If an experienced property business entrepreneur is feeling like this, don't worry if you are as well!

But remember:

A goal without a plan is just a wish!!!

It's the plan that makes the wish come true.

That is the beauty of the STOMP methodology, it turns your goals for each part of your business into a workable plan that you can do something with. It helps you with the tasks of deciding which bits are working ON and which are working IN your business. But it also allows you to consider all aspects of your business when planning, and not just those that you find easiest – Remember the Eisenhower's Matrix? You need to be aware of the difference between working ON and IN your business. The planning process is a big part of working ON your business. It enables you to identify those Important and/or urgent action tasks.

Every year, least you should review your previous year to see what went well, what could be improved and whether you are still heading in the direction you want. Then you can decide your destination for the next year, how much you want your business to grow and you can flex your plan accordingly. This becomes your vision for the next year.

But just yearly planning like this is just not effective. Why should this be so when you have considered your vision, the direction you want to go in and the growth you want to achieve? Well, it is because a year is a long time and you can put off doing any major actions for a long time and it will still not impact upon your yearly plan until it is too late and it has become impossible to achieve.

Procrastination is the devil to an entrepreneur so guard against it. It will stop you working towards your vision, it will slowly creep up on you without you noticing and when you review the year you will not be anywhere near where you wanted to be. You may even have changed direction completely without even consulting your vision. You would be surprised how often this happens. The plans are produced but they then just sit on your shelf and are never looked at again.

Just think about all those New Year's Resolutions that people make?

What happens to them in February?

Or even by January 10th?

See what I mean? This happens to business plans as well that are not:

a) Written down
b) Implemented
c) Reviewed at regular intervals throughout the year

This is where 90 day planning comes into its own. It's a bit like making New Year's Resolutions about your business development but renewing them every quarter!

Why a 90 Day Plan? Well it enables you to:

- Break the big goals that you want to achieve for the year into small, manageable, achievable steps.
- It forces you into action – but action ON and not just IN your business!
- It keeps your business responsive to change as you reassess and review the plan and the external environment every quarter.
- It gives you something to share as your vision with your team
- It is easy to do and can be worked into any busy schedule.

- Humans achieve lots just after writing down a goal and making plans towards that goal. Do this frequently and regularly and you help stop procrastination in its tracks because you are not accountable to yourself (or a coach if you are writing this with them).

Now, you do still need your big vision of where you want your business to be in 1, 3 or 5 years down the line. This should be grounded in your values as discussed in Chapter 2. This vision should be big and possibly a bit scary for you! This is good. We should be excited by our visions and they will they push you out of your comfort zone. Many business coaches talk about "Big Hairy Goals", they claim that you need to double your goals to make them scary! I will leave that up to you! But think big here. Why?

Shoot for the moon, if you miss, you'll land among the stars!!

You might as well plan for being big rather than planning for average, nobody wants to be average. You are not in property to be average; you may have given up a lucrative career, time with your family or friends or opportunities to pursue this dream, so pursue it with vigour and plan big!

When researching for this book, I discovered that lots of people think business planning should be detailed, full of financial predictions and used mostly for gaining investment. Now, there is a place for a business plan that looks like this and a bank may well ask for your business plan when discussing opening bank accounts and accessing overdrafts etc., however a business plan should be a flexible, useable document that guides your day-to-day decision making, so if it is too big and cumbersome it will not get used so it is just a waste of time.

Most of our investors have been more interested in investing in property-specific deals or just want to invest in us as people, rather than looking at detailed financial predictions. Our 'plan' is our business strategy and it is written on one page! We can share the plan and that vision with anybody because it is easy enough for us to understand, it is not over complicated or intricate. It is just plain simple English on just one page for our three-five year planning. It is a high-level vision for our business so it doesn't need to be detailed.

Now don't get me wrong, it may look simple and be very easy to explain to others – the point of the strategy is to share it – but it is backed up by detailed research and understanding of our businesses and the sectors that they operate in. It's just that that detail does not have to be in a report – the strategy or plan only needs to be high level.

The whole point I am making when planning is to KISS

KEEP IT SIMPLE, STUPID!

Both the strategy and the 90-day plan need to be simple to understand, produce, review, revise and use. The 90-day plan needs to have:

- A few key goals for each section of your business
- Each goal needs to attainable within the 90 day period
- Each goal needs to be specific
- Each goal needs to be measurable – otherwise, how will you know whether you have succeeded or not?

But I have got carried away with myself a bit here. Let us start at the beginning and look at the business strategy, as that is the first port of call when planning.

We only briefly looked at it in Chapter 2. We will show you how each section of our Strategy on a Page works, the template can be downloaded from our "Recommendations" section on our website www.business-academy.co.uk

Business Strategy

So a business strategy should be your high-level road map of where you want to get to. This should help you stay on track and stop you getting 'lost' on your journey through your business. Imagine it is the SatNav in your phone, constantly checking where you are against where you want to be going, helping you make small adjustments because of what is happening outside the car (this is the economic environment in this analogy). That is what your yearly business strategy, and then your 90-day plan, should be doing for you, giving you slight adjustments to ensure that you reach your desired location on time and relaxed, not frazzled and stressed!

This is why it is so important to have a destination – a vision – of where you want your business to be, so that the SatNav (your 90-day plan) can work out the best route forward. You should always be reviewing progress along the way (at least every 30 days) because things will knock you off course – there are always road works to get round, or heavy traffic to avoid or that lorry that got stuck under the bridge to avoid.

How do you go about considering and then writing this strategy?

This is a little bit of magic that I will now share with you!

1. Identify the "purpose of being" for your business (from Chapter 2). You would normally have up to five but no more

2. From that, identify your values (from Chapter 2). You would normally have up to five but no more.

3. Don't skip steps 1 & 2. Go back to Chapter 2 if you have.

4. From your purpose of being and your values you can identify your vision for your business.. Really, don't skip steps 1 & 2 because they should underpin your vision for your business (from chapter 2) and without it nothing else will make sense.

5. Identify what makes your business different – your unique selling proposition (more in a minute on this.)

6. You should then be able to identify the niche or gap in the market that you are aiming to fill with your products.

7. Add in the company promise – what will you, as a business, promise to do.

8. Have you done steps 1 & 2 – are you realising how important they are yet!!?

All of the above will give you fantastic information for you to use in any promotion that you are going to do. It helps if you can have a clear vision which is underpinned by your purpose and values, have a clear niche (a problem that you want to solve with your products) and to have a company promise. These are really powerful words that should motivate you, attract others to you and help you with your marketing messages.

Let's go through all of this individually in detail

Reason for Being (Why are you in business?)

This first section answers the question <u>Why</u> does your business exist?   It must align with your higher purpose. If not then the business will not serve you and your needs and you will not put the required work in to make it a success.

If you want to read more on this then there are recommending readings on our website(www.business-academy.co.uk) under 'Recommendations'.

Opportunity

What opportunity have you identified in the market that your business will meet? There has to be an opportunity otherwise you are just hoping things will work.

Service & Value

How are you going to serve the market to meet the opportunity? What value will you give that means people will buy from you rather than anyone else. Remember that value is perceived by the customer, so good quality cheap accommodation is just as valid as high end, high priced, all singing all dancing accommodation. It all depends on your market opportunity.

Passion

Without a passion for what you are doing you will get fed up with the work required. Are you passionate about helping the homeless, interior design, providing a legacy for your family etc. etc.... Remember the Passion Circle from Chapter 2? If you have skill and there is a gap in the market, but you are not passionate, then you will end up in a passionless job, just imagine for a minute creating a passionless business AND spending years doing it to yourself!

Financial reward

What level of financial reward do you want? Do you want £10K a month; £1M of income producing assets; to ensure your children can take a £2K income so they can pursue their interests or will all profits go into your pension so that you can retire comfortably and early? Only you can answer this.

Lifestyle

What sort of lifestyle will the business give you? We recommend you think long and hard about this since it is very easy to say that "I want to travel the world and have a fast car and only work one day a week etc." Your lifestyle choices will require you to set up a business structure and select investment tactics that will support your choices so choose wisely and have a meaning that is personal to you.

You will notice that at this stage we have not considered what type of properties you will be buying; how you will control them or what property income producing tactics (property strategy) you will use. These come much later and they must serve you and the reason your business exists. If you think about this too early you will end up serving your tactics rather than your tactics serving you and you too will become a tired landlord.

Values (How will you operate?)

This section answers the question <u>How</u> will the business operate?

Every business has its own values. Just think about some that you know. For example, Innocent Smoothies and Coca Cola. Both are drinks companies but they have very different values. Innocent Smoothies core value is "Do no harm" whereas Coca Colas is all about "leadership, collaboration, integrity, accountability, passion, diversity, and quality.

For you and your business to be congruent you need to instil your values into your business. Can you imagine an environmental campaigner creating an oil company? Of course not, it would be totally against their values. So build something that aligns with your values.

But do you know what your values are? Re-read Chapter 1 & 2 and go to our website www.business-academy.co.uk for recommendations on further reading. This will give you a real insight into what drives you. This personal driving force must be the same as what drives your business otherwise; again, you will not do the work that you need to, to make your business a success.

Vision - Expression of Purpose *(What?)*

- Only now do we set out your vision for your business by answering the question What is the business going to do?
- This is your vision for what you are going to build. Make it as vivid and exciting as you can. It must excite you reading it!

- What are you going to offer?

- How will the business be regarded by others?

- How will it operate? Are you going to do it all yourself or will you build a team around you?

- How will you decide who you work with?

There is no real format to this section. It is whatever you need to express the vision of your business and what it will look like when it is done. This could be in one, three or five years time.

Unique Selling Proposition

Let's just spend a few minutes going over what we mean by USP, just so that you understand it and can, therefore, use it.

There are a lot of properties out there for sale and rent. Why should somebody choose yours above anybody else's? Some applicants are just lazy and will want any type of accommodation that they can afford – there is a marketplace for the bog-standard accommodation as well. But how do you attract better applicants?

We are constantly being asked how we achieve such high rents in our shared houses. Typically we are 40-

50% higher than the published averages. Agents are always telling us, 'you will not get that rent in this town', and yet we do. People are always saying to us, 'you need to have en suites to get those rents in this town,' and yet we have almost no en suites in our portfolio and certainly wouldn't try to squeeze them in. We are always having agents say, 'you will not fill an 8 bed in the town centre', and yet we have waiting lists to move in. WHY?

Answers:

- We have a clear USP that is in all our promotional material.

- We attract good tenants because paying more for a product means not everybody can afford it so we have well paid professional tenants.

- The good tenants look after the properties well so that we have fewer maintenance visits.

- The good tenants recommend us to friends and family.

- Tenants return to us – we have graduates come to do their training and rent from us for 9 months. They then get a job at the company and call us first to see what is available before even checking the competition – why is that?

Isn't it worth spending time on your values, your purpose, your vision and your USP so that you can also do the same? Here's another bit of magic – this works for ALL businesses, not just property businesses. If you can identify a niche that has a problem and solve that problem, then you will have customers for your products! That is what big businesses do, that is how they come up with an innovation, which is how they make their millions. Honest, it's not a secret really.

So here are five steps to help identifying and use your USP might be:

1. List the features or benefits that are unique about your product or service – now remember you are also offering a service, not just somewhere to live! We operate a paperless, systemised on-boarding process which we use as part of our marketing message. So it might not only be your product (your accommodation) but it could be how you do things.

2. What emotional need is being met by your product or service? Emotions sell products, meeting a customer's emotional needs means they are more

likely to buy from you. Part of our USP is that we are a green business, and this attracts tenants with the same values.

3. Identify aspects of your product or service that your competitors can not imitate – now, this is more difficult with properties, but we, do this through our property designs, each shared house is unique, quirky and 'homely', this is difficult for competitors to replicate.

4. Create phrases about your USP that are short, clear and concise – this is the important bit, it helps with your promotional copy to have the USP told in a short, clear and concise way, so that everybody can understand it. You can then put it everywhere – websites, social media profiles, SpareRoom adverts, investment packs – everywhere.

5. Answer your customer's question "What's in it for me"? Remember it should all be about the customer, so when talking to potential tenants, tell them what is in it for them!!! That way you are attracting them and attracting the potential tenants that you would want to have.

This might seem like hard work but believe us; it helps to focus your business strategy, which will focus your 90-day plans for moving your business forward. It will also give you a really good copy to use in promotional material. So, it is worth the effort you put in.

Defined Market Space (Who? & Where?)

So you have identified your USP, but is there a gap in the market? Is there that defined market space for what you want to offer? This is the <u>Who</u> will you sell to and <u>Where</u> will you be questions. Really important questions for any business, but especially for property businesses).

Here's how to identify any gaps:

1. Trends – identify any trends that are happening in the property industry generally. They may not have hit your area yet, but industry trends are a good way of identifying any gaps you might be able to exploit.
2. Holidays or experience – is there anything you have noticed whilst travelling that you thought was better than the way we do things here? Is there anything in your past that could influence your experience? Red

Door Homes has William (our son) as the CEO, this is crucial for us because he is our target customer, how many boards have actual examples of their target customer on them directing the business? We used William's really bad experience in houses he lived in to make something better and identify our gap in the market.

3. Add a twist to what is already offered – you don't need to re-invent the wheel, as discussed in USP, you can just do something a little different in the way you deliver your products (e.g. paperless), and that can give you a gap in the market.

4. Customer feedback – if you already have properties, why don't you ask your current tenants how you could improve, or what would make their lives easier? As they are the ones living in or buying your accommodation they should be able to help, use any resource you can. Sending a quick survey via MailChimp is a really good way of gauging response to the product you are offering and discovering what you could do differently.

5. Ask Agents – they have the local knowledge, even if it is only, 'this is what is round here' you can always do something different!

Company Promise

Why include a company promise in a business strategy document? Well if you make a promise you have to keep it, especially if it is a pinky promise!!! Now, most business books will probably not include a company promise here. I have nicked the idea from Derri Llywelyn Davies - The Strategy Man – if you ever get a chance to hear his talks, please go, he is brilliant. I like the idea of putting in a promise because it does mean you have to keep it.

This is one of the most powerful parts of your USP and can really set you apart from your competition. What promise does your business make to your customers?

The promise focuses your mind for writing promotional copy and also when making major or minor decisions. It's a quick sanity check – will we be keeping our company promise if we do something this way?

So, although it might seem like another step, it is a valuable one, and because it is the last step in creating your business strategy, it should be underpinned by everything that comes before it. Everything like your values, your vision, your purpose, your USP and the gap you have identified.

A great example from the 70's and 80's is FedEx.

"When It Absolutely, Positively Has to Be There Overnight"

Quite a promise to keep but it really said a lot to their customers.

Exercise 14

Identifying your Unique Selling Proposition – work your way through these questions:

1. Understand your target customer (we did this in Chapter 8). Make a list of what you know about your target customer. Try to get at least 20 things that you know about them. You may have to do this for several groups of customers because we have 'potential tenants' as well as 'R2R landlords' and of course 'investors'. The same research needs to be carried out for every target audience. After all, the message may need to be slightly different for each group.

2. Make a list of all the needs that your product (or the way you offer it) can meet. These are your potential USPs

3. Then, use these to identify your competitive advantage – what you do that your competitors can't replicate? Remember, this can be the way that you do something, or the products that you offer.

4. Carry out market research – You could always just ask existing tenants if they are your target customer?

Does your USP still match the needs and wants of your target audience?

5. Identify the industry trends that are happening – not just in your location, but nationally or internationally, because you could replicate it or do it slightly differently.

6. Check your results, does it have a strong, clear benefit for those you are targeting? Can you deliver on what you have promised?

7. Use this USP in the Promotional material – everywhere you talk about your business use this USP. This includes adverts, social media, websites and business cards.

You should now have a clearer idea of your USP, and it should be underpinned by the values and vision for your business.

The Details In Your Plan - Tactics:

Now that you have your business strategy set out you can begin to decide how you intend to go about delivering that strategy. This is where you set out your business tactics or actions for the next 90 and 30 days. This is where your property Strategies come into play.

- How will you find the properties and the money required?

- Who are you going to work with?

- How will you operate the business and how will you manage the properties?

- How much money do you need to make, how much do you need to find to deliver your vision and from whom?

- How will you advertise for tenants?

- How will you find investors?

There are many tactics that could be considered here but you need to focus on the ones that will make a difference to your business. Everybody will complete this section in a different way but don't forget to consider all the work you have done in the previous sections. Do the tactics that you are planning to use support the strategy and the way you want your business to run. Your plan must be congruent across your strategy and your tactics otherwise they will conflict and you cannot do anything without breaking part of your plan.

Core Long Term Tactics

Imagine your business in five years' time. What does it look like? This is where you get to set out your vision for the long term aims of your business.

We break the elements of a property business into 5 distinct areas and we use the acronym STOMP. This ensures we consider all the required areas for our property business and remind us to work ON and not IN our business. After all, you would STOMP ON your business you would not STOMP IN your business!

Sourcing - How will you source your properties and investors? How many? How much?

Team - Who do you need in your team? Will they be employed or outsourced

Operations - How will you run the operations? In house or outsourced? Using what systems

Money - What will your income be, what will the company turnover and profit be etc.

Promotion - How will you promote the business to both tenants and investors?

Consider all areas of the business using STOMP so that you ensure a balanced development of the business. This is why each area has its own chapter so you can understand this better.

Annual Tactics

Five year targets are too far ahead to be of any use in your day to day business so imagine your business this time next year. What do you want to have achieved? How many properties? How much money do you need both personal income and investors? What systems are you going to have in place? What team members are you going to have?

Again, consider all areas of the business using STOMP so that you ensure a balanced development of the business.

Goals

These are the key measurables in your business and should be reviewed regularly. Only you will know which are the most appropriate Key Growth indicators for your business but for many property businesses they will include Revenue, Net Profit, Gross Profit, Personal Income, Number of Rooms, Number of Properties, Value of properties under management.

There is a whole chapter on this in Chapter 10 if you want to flick forward, just remember to come back here!

Your long term goals give you an idea of the measurable elements of what you are looking to achieve in 5 years. But a lot can happen in 5 years so we bring that back to what are your goals for this year since that is more easy to believe and to see your progress towards. However one year is also a long time so we then break it down to quarters, then months and then weeks to give you what you need to be doing today to realise the vision for your business.

How to use your Business Strategy now that you have it

If you look at the two pages of the business strategy template from our website www.business-academy.co.uk you will see that they are very different.

The first page sets out your vision for the business. This will not change very often but is essential to keep you on track to delivering your vision.

The second page set out the tactics for how your business will deliver that vision. This will change all of the time as you progress through set up to adolescence and on to maturity in your business. It is the key document that helps you to determine what you need to be doing this quarter, this month, this week, today in your business.

So to use your business strategy correctly there is no point in writing it and then putting it in a drawer. It needs to be put somewhere you see it all the time. In our house we have a magic kitchen cupboard where we put pictures and descriptions of everything we want in life. This keeps the things we want at the forefront of our mind. We update the tactics page at least monthly and we use the strategy page and the tactics page as part of our monthly and 90 day business planning sessions to keep us on track and help us deliver the wonderful life we have envisioned for ourselves. We suggest you do to.

90 Day Planning

So, you now have your company strategy, hopefully, you should be enthused by your work so far. It should help build the future you want and also the business that you want.

Now, 90-day plans should be really simple (just like the business strategy), however it is frequently over-complicated by including things that are not relevant, or that should be on the business strategy for the year, not the next 90 days. We choose 90 days because you can split the year up into nice, easy chunks.

Those 90 days make great planning time scales. After all, it gives you time to get a real good chunk of work done in a particular area, because not everything you put down can be done immediately! It is also a nice timescale for remembering and reviewing. It is not too far ahead so you can still stay very flexible if major changes happen out of the blue, but it does give you a clear action plan that should allow you to achieve your yearly targets. Remember it will help eliminate procrastination from your business!

90-day planning can also help to alleviate the overwhelming feeling that some entrepreneurs feel as it gives a clear plan and working through a plan makes us feel better and more in control! Anxiety and stress can drain the excitement out of an entrepreneur and, therefore, their businesses as well; to stop this overwhelming feeling do some 90-day planning.

Easy Process:

1. Goal – what do you want to achieve for this 90-day session? Now, here is the clever part, we have

already said it but worth saying again. You should have a maximum of three goals for EACH OF THE STOMP areas of your business. This is the beauty of STOMP, it allows you to look at parts of the business where you may have been too anxious to consider or unaware that it needs looking at before! Looking at each area of STOMP every 90 days will help you build a balanced business.

2. Resource – have you got the resources to do what you want to achieve? Now, be honest here. You cannot scale or grow a business without some finance, even if this money is just there to outsource current jobs you are doing to free up your time.

3. Commitment – well this is easy, you are committed to your goals, aren't you? If they are in line with your values and your vision you should be. But here are some difficult questions – is your team committed to your goals? Your business partner? Your life partner? Your investors? This is where sharing a vision, even if it is just the vision of what will be achieved in the next 90 days, is important – it gets others committed to your goals as well as yourself, and that is a very powerful concept. This

also encourages accountability between the people you have shared your commitment with. This all helps to eliminate that procrastinating feeling again.

4. Plan – obvious really, in a section all about planning, but write it down, a plan written down is more likely to be achieved than one which is not. Writing it down and putting it somewhere prominent keeps it in your line of vision and makes you do something!

5. Challenges – whilst doing the planning process you will come across challenges, it is really good if you can identify these and then talk them through with someone. This is where business partners, life partners or business coaches come into their own. Having a sounding board allows you to come up with solutions. Try the 20 in 20 method!

20 In 20 Solution Method

If you have got a particularly hard problem that you need to solve, get together with whoever normally listens to you and have a 20 in 20 session. Everybody comes up with 20 solutions to the problem in 20 minutes. Now the 20 minutes is important because you need to give your brain time to work; the 20 solutions are important because by the time you are getting to solution 16-20 you will probably have found the ones you want to do. You should do this as an individual exercise and then come together to discuss everybody's solutions or do it in a group until you have come up with 20 solutions in your 20 minutes.

We have used both methods and we have found the group works best for us as we spark off each other. But, I know of other businesses that do it individually and come together to choose the right one. There is no right or wrong way, it is just a way of getting loads of solutions out of your head, talking about them and getting them on to paper.

The STOMP 90-day planning tools are a big help here with the actual writing down of the actions. Once you have the actions, you can allocate responsibilities for completing them and decide which resources everybody needs. Accountability is therefore written into the planning and reviewing process – a very powerful tool to help you achieve your vision.

Do you see how this helps you with a framework to plan and work ON and IN your business? It is all to easy to be working on a deal, get it, refurbish it, tenant it, only to look round and find that you have only grown by one property. You don't have the funnel for marketing or sourcing. You may have run out of cash or be wondering where all the money has gone. To grow big you need to have those funnels, which means concentrating on Sourcing, Promotion, and Money to make the current refurb and the tenants efficient you need to concentrate on Operation – does that make sense? They are all interlinked towards growing your business, but they can be planned separately.

All this planning of every aspect of your business should also make individual projects easier to manager and enable much more accurate project management to occur. There is a module on project management on our website if you need some more guidance here www.business-academy.co.uk.

30 Day Plan

On the STOMP 90 day planning sheets you will see that the 90-day plans are on the left-hand side, then each month has its tasks. These tasks are the ones that need to be completed so that the larger goals are done. The 90-day plans lead to the yearly plan in the same way. As there are three months in every quarter you can decide at what point you carry out the work.

Spending time every month deciding:

a) Is this course of action still correct after reviewing your plan?

b) What actions need to be completed in the next 30 days to get you closer to achieving the plan?

c) Who will be responsible for each action?

Do this for each of the STOMP areas – there should be no more than three per section because our poor brains can't cope with much more! This is a maximum of 15 key actions that need to be completed within the next 30 days.

Again, this is where accountability comes in, as this plan will be reviewed in 30 days, then again in another 30 days, then again in another 30 days – it becomes embarrassing if you have not made progress!

Weekly Actions

Now every week, look at the plan and decide what you can get completed this week. Be honest with yourself and look at your schedule. You should be finding a minimum of 30 minutes a day to work ON your business, or, if you need chunks of time an hour every other day. If you can manage 90 minutes a day you would motor through your actions, but sometimes this is not possible. Don't be too hard on yourself, but do allocate time every day for improving your business.

What is important is that you schedule time in your diary, block it out and don't let anything interfere with it. This is hard, very hard. But if you keep the plan in your sights – and this is one of the few pieces of paper that we print out and have with us at all times – it helps. Being able to see your 90-day plan and 30 plan in one place, helps to keep you focussed.

This is why we have designed the plan on one page and with a maximum of three actions per section – it keeps us focussed, and is simple and achievable. Remember the goals can be a stretch (your big hairy goals), but the steps towards them need to be achievable, this planning methodology is a way to keep them achievable and to achieve them!

Word of Warning

Every person I have ever known who does 90-day planning –including ourselves – overestimates how much work can be done in the first month, completes some of the second month's actions and only a few of the third month's actions. Does this matter?

Well if you plan, at least you are making steps forward towards your end vision, if you don't consider what needs to be done and don't plan it, then you would probably not get the work half-completed at all, let alone thought about! So, we do except that we overestimate and don't normally complete everything in the third month, but that is why we review it every month and 90 days!

Reviewing your plan is important, it means that you can identify what needs to be done going forward into the next 30 days and what is still relevant or if the vision or goals have changed. Without this review process, then the plan would be inflexible and not much good to anybody.

Review

So, reviews of the actions, tasks and plans should happen every week. Ideally just check where you are, especially every month to decide how far through the tasks you are and every 90 days to check that the plan is still relevant. Every year you should have a big review to check how far you've come and where you want to be in the next year.

When should you review in the year?

This is completely down to you. Some people like to review the year in January for obvious reasons, but September is also a good review point. Any time that comes after a holiday. Why? When we are away on holidays (summer or Christmas) our brains relax and wonder and create, so that when we get back home, we are frustrated by things not being as we want them, this propels us into action. Honestly, it a well-known fact!

Tools to Help

There is a One Page Strategy template available on our website www.business-academy.co.uk

Exercise 15

Use the STOMP 90-day planning tool to start to plan the actions you need to do in your business for the next 90 days and every 30 days of that period.

Print out your plan and keep it with you – tick things off once they are achieved and get that sense of achievement when you have reached your goals!!!

Tools on the website www.business-academy.co.uk

Chapter 10

Business Growth Indicators

Quotation

"I am prepared for the worst, but hope for the best"

Benjamin Disraeli, British Statesman 1804-1881

"Rule No 1 - Don't lose any money

Rule No 2 - See rule No 1"

Warren Buffet

Chapter 10 – Business Growth Indicators

As Brian Tracy (an American-Canadian public speaker) said

"Money is hard to earn and easy to lose. Guard yours with care"

This chapter is all about understanding how your money is earned by the indicators in your business so that you don't end up losing any of it! Guard that growth, understand it so that you can replicate it or change direction if it is not working.

How do you know if you have achieved the growth and scale that you are looking for? Well, there should be some measurements in place so that you can see how far towards goals you have travelled or have yet to travel. These indicators of your growth are what you measure in your business. Every business is different, so you will have to decide what yours should be. KGIs are an essential part of your management skill set since they enable you to track and show if you are making positive steps towards your business strategy goals.

Property businesses are slightly different from other sectors, but the measurement is still important. If you spend £600 to get a tenant to sign a tenancy agreement it might show that you are not efficient in your on-boarding process. You may ask "how will I spend £600, that's a lot?" but when you add everything up – advertising in lots of places; time spent responding to adverts; time spent on organising all viewings; time spent on the viewings; travel time to the viewings; time spent doing references and paperwork; time spent checking tenants, it is very easy to spend £600 to get one tenant who may be paying £375 per month – so you are into month three before you have broken even with each tenant on a six month AST! See, this is a valuable measurement to look at to ensure that the on-boarding system is as efficient as possible.

Your businesses metrics are important and should play a key role in the management of your business. Remember, you can also measure things that seem un-measurable like 'feelings'. This is can be done on a scale

"On a scale of 1-10, 1 being poor and 10 being fantastic

How do you feel your communication with the team has been this month?

1 2 3 4 5 6 7 8 9 10"

This makes even intangible concepts measurable and that means you can see improvements on a monthly or quarterly basis. (So long as you are honest with yourselves of course!).

You could also track the performance of a goal expressed as a percentage. For example, how do you track the purchase of a property when it can take months? Well, use a 'percentage complete' KGI. For example, if you have only just had the offer accepted, you would only be 5% complete, however, if you were due to exchange tomorrow you would 99% complete. Percentages help our brain compare things, so this is a really good measure if you are bringing lots of projects in at once.

A good plan will use between 5-7 KGI, this is because we can't concentrate on too many things. Not all indicators are important to your business all the time, some will come and go as your business develops. When choosing your KGI you need to consider:

- The measurement – every KGI needs to be measurable in some way, what are you measuring? Making them more expressive is better, rather than just "number of new tenants" say "number of new tenants this month"

- The target – every KGI should be associated with a growth goal from your strategy or 90-day plan. This needs to have a time frame – "we need to achieve ten new rooms available in the next six months". The goal and target timeframes should match each other

- The measurement and the target should be the same, i.e. they should both be numbers or percentages, don't try to have a percentage as a measurement and a number as a target it will confuse you!

- A data source – you need to know where the data is coming from and know that it is reliable and accurate

- Reporting frequency – not all KGIs will need to be reviewed weekly, you need to decide when you want to review them. You also need to be able to get the data in a timely fashion for reporting as well! Some will be quarterly or monthly or even weekly, if it is a particularly time-sensitive goal.

Some KGIs will be for your long term strategy, they are for 1-5 years measurements so will probably need to be reviewed annually. Some will be for the year and you should keep an eye on them to ensure that you will achieve your goals on time. Some will be just for the quarter because that is where your focus is. If you have just completed a new HMO or a block of flats then "Units Available" will suddenly be high, so all measurements need to be considered within the context of what your business is doing.

Some KGI's will be an expression of comparison with last year or last period's figures. What is the percentage increase in the room? What is the percentage increase in profit or rent roll? You may need to check out Basic Maths for Property Businesses on our website if you are not sure about how to calculate some of these figures. They are easy but getting them right will enable you to have accurate comparisons.

Examples:

Here are some examples of KGI you could use although this is not definitive.

Source

- Value of property owned
- No. of investor meetings
- No. of offers put on properties
- No. of offers accepted

Team

- Quality of new employees
- Headcount
- Staff efficiency
- Team achievements
- VA efficiency
- ROI of training
- Workforce retention
- Cost of the workforce
- Employee satisfaction index
- Number of contractors

Operations

- Voids
- No. of rooms (properties) added
- No. of rooms reserved
- No. of rooms sold

- Tenant satisfaction index
- Average time to fill a room/property
- Application received per room sold

Money

- Growth in revenue (money coming in)
- Operational cash flow
- Investment needed
- Rent overdue
- Cost of getting a tenant
- Cost of managing debt
- Annual profit
- Cash reserves
- Turnover per month
- Rent Roll per month

Promotion

- Number of hits on adverts
- Conversion from advert to tenant
- Number of new tenants
- Cost of advertising
- Number of landlords letters sent out

Why are KGIs Important?

Big businesses track their KGIs on a Scorecard and review it frequently so that adjustments can be made if they are straying away from their targets. Why shouldn't you? Remember, you want to scale your business, and that means using the methods that big businesses use. So, identifying, tracking and reviewing your KGIs are a key management skill to ensure that you are growing in the right direction and that you are actually achieving the vision for your business.

Your KGIs are there to track the performance and health of your business, they allow you to make critical adjustments to your plans so that you can achieve your vision. Your KGIs, therefore, provide a benchmark for you to track your businesses growth and determine what growth you have achieved. It also enables you to be more objective in your decision making and possibly a little bit more scientific in the process of making decisions. This could mean the difference between making decisions based upon 'your gut instinct' only, or, making decisions based on sound information AND 'your gut instinct' combined.

Never ignore your gut instinct because it is there for a reason, it is your values nudging you in the right direction (normally). But underpinning this with some key measures from your business will give you much better quality decisions.

The KGI's can also be called your 'Dashboard' as it is like the dashboard of your car. It gives you vital information so that you can take action to alter your course if needed.

As you grow and have other people doing the day to day work you need measures in place to ensure that they are doing the right thing so they drive their behaviour in the direction that you want. I had an interesting conversation with one person (not property) who said they had had to get rid of their bookkeeper because they were not chasing debtors (people who owed the business money) enough for their liking. They therefore decided to go back to doing all the bookkeeping themselves. This seems crazy, as all the time and effort put into training this person has gone to waste. Surely a better response would have been to have some targets for the bookkeeper, monitor those targets and have a conversation with them? Possibly on a weekly basis.

This conversation would not have been hard – "let's have a chat on Friday's about how much debt you have been able to chase through this week". Doing this weekly would then have driven the bookkeeper to understand the following behaviour:

a) What was a priority – don't assume team members know or share your priorities!

b) That it was such a high priority it was going to be reviewed weekly so they should get on with it

c) That their performance was being monitored and, therefore, this was a really important target for the manager

This conversation would have given the bookkeeper a better idea of what their job was about, and the owner could have shared their vision with them so that they felt part of something, instead of just a cog that didn't fit. These things matter as you get bigger and you want to grow and scale your business, so they should be important now. Getting it right at the beginning is easier / cheaper / more efficient than reinventing things later!

Tools to Help:

There is a module on the website www.business-academy.co.uk which helps you identify what your Key Growth Indicators should be and how to track them.

Exercise 16

Identify some KGIs that you could use. Consider some for:

- The long term plan (1+ years)
- The medium plan (1 year)
- The 90-day plan

They may be different!

Consider:

- The measurements you will use and what timeframes you will put on them
- The target you want to achieve and the time frame
- The data source and where and how you will get the information
- When you want to report each KGI – at the yearly review, monthly review or quarterly review

Put them into the 'Tactics' section of the Plan.

Chapter 11

Conclusion

Quotation

"Most people end up owning a business by accident. Therefore, they don't usually have a thought process and a strategic plan in place"

Carol Roth, American Author, 1973 -

Chapter 11 – Conclusion

Well, what have I learned?

You should have learned a little bit from reading this book – even if it is only that you need a bit more information about the different sections of the book.

So here's the last exercise for you

Exercise 17

On a scale of 1-5 (1 being not good, 5 being brilliant) please rate yourself:

Vision, how well do you	
• Know what you want your business to look like next year?	1 2 3 4 5 1 2 3 4 5
• Share this vision	1 2 3 4 5
• Talk about this vision	
Communication, how well do you communicate:	
• your vision to yourself	1 2 3 4 5
• your vision to stakeholders	1 2 3 4 5
• your requirements to your power team	1 2 3 4 5
• your needs to your business partner	1 2 3 4 5
• your needs to your life partner (if different)	1 2 3 4 5

Time management, how well do you	
	1 2 3 4 5
• manage your time	1 2 3 4 5
• become the most effective you can be	1 2 3 4 5
• plan your time	1 2 3 4 5
• plan your business	1 2 3 4 5
• plan your actions	
Business awareness, how well do you	
• know what your business needs	1 2 3 4 5
	1 2 3 4 5
• understand the needs of your business as it grows	1 2 3 4 5
• how to grow your business	1 2 3 4 5
• how to get to where you want to get to	1 2 3 4 5
• work on and not in your business	
Problem-solving, how well do you:	
	1 2 3 4 5

• solve problems effectively	1 2 3 4 5
• have the same or similar problems occurring	1 2 3 4 5
• learn from mistakes	1 2 3 4 5
• delegate	1 2 3 4 5
• outsource	1 2 3 4 5
• use your time	
Totals	

If you scored 115-125 – well done you don't need to read anything else, you know everything and already have the skills to build a big, successful business. If you scored between 80-110 – then you could do with pointers to become more effective and grow your business. If you scored below 80 – you could do with a little help in understanding how to grow and manage your business so that it can be the success you want it to be. All of this is learnable, you just need to be ready to listen.

Conclusion

In this book I can only scratch the surface, but if you are serious about growing a successful business that will be around for the long term, then you need to know this stuff.

You should now be a little clearer about:

- How to identify what your vision for your business should be
- That business can be split up into different sections
- What marketing is
- What a marketing funnel is and how you can use it for different areas of your business
- How identifying your ideal customers can allow you to add significant value to your product and your business
- Why you should systemise your business and what it can do for your business
- How to systemise your business
- The pros and cons of outsourcing or employing somebody
- If you are employing somebody, what you need to do
- Sharing your vision with employees and outsourcers
- The key terminology used by accountants
- The difference between profit and cash and what it means for your business

- The legal requirements for a limited company for HMRC and Companies House
- What the planning process is
- How to write a One Page Strategy for your business
- What Key Growth Indicators you could use to help you measure your success

That is quite a lot to pack into such a small space! If there is one thing we think you should concentrate on it is the vision for your business because as this will help you with your marketing, how you operate your business, whose help you need to bring that vision about and how you will fund it!

Chapter 12

Next Steps

Quotation

"They who would learn to fly one day must first learn to stand and walk and run and climb and dance; one cannot fly into flying"

Friedrich Nietzsche, German Philosopher, 1844-1900

Chapter 12 – Next Steps

We at The Business Academy offer fantastic training and support programs to help you scale your business sustainably and securely. We can do this because:

a) We have been there, done it and bought the T-Shirt!

b) We have done it over multiple industry sectors

c) We have a track record of helping others grow and develop themselves and their businesses.

d) We know your pain and know a solution to help.

There are a range of modules designed as progression tools to deepen your learning and understanding of the topics in this book plus loads of other topics that we have not had the space to go into here. There is something to help every aspect of your business, because if we don't know the answer then we know somebody who does!

There are modules designed for three different levels of business depending upon what you want to achieve. These levels are:

- Business 101

A specifically designed set of on-line modules and support for you (or a team member) to be able to understand and do the day to day work in your business more efficiently and more effectively. It is jammed packed with lots of information, tips and recommendations to help you with the business basics. Each module can be purchased on an 'as you need it' basis enabling you to tailor training as and when you need it.

- Business Owner Manager Level

Specifically designed set of on-line modules, on-going support and mastermind events for you to take the first steps away from the day to day running of your business, systemise it and take back control. This will make it far more efficient and effective and enable you to grow beyond you doing all the doings constantly! This level will enable you to free up your time and energy so that you can grow your business.

- Entrepreneurial Level

Specifically designed set of on-line modules, on-going weekly and monthly support, on-going coaching and mastermind events all designed to increase your understanding of yourself, your business, its place in the environment etc. These are designed to facilitate you becoming an entrepreneur, stepping away from the day to day running of your business and into working purely ON your business. This level is the ultimate learning and support package for entrepreneurs to learn to become the conductor of their business so that you can truly scale your business.

If you are interested in any of the above levels then just contact us via:

Email: Support@business-academy.co.uk

Website: www.business-academy.co.uk

Facebook: https://www.facebook.com/the.business.academy.uk

LinkedIn: https://www.linkedin.com/company/business-academy-uk

Printed in Germany
by Amazon Distribution
GmbH, Leipzig

18522241R00139